D0842929

# Sensible Decisions

# Sensible Decisions

## Issues of Rational Decision in Personal Choice and Public Policy

Nicholas Rescher

ROWMAN & LITTLEFIELD PUBLISHERS, INC.
*Lanham • Boulder • New York • Oxford*

ROWMAN & LITTLEFIELD PUBLISHERS, INC.

Published in the United States of America
by Rowman & Littlefield Publishers, Inc.
A Member of the Rowman & Littlefield Publishing Group
4501 Forbes Boulevard, Suite 200, Lanham, Maryland 20706
www.rowmanlittlefield.com

PO Box 317
Oxford
OX2 9RU, UK

British Library Cataloguing in Publication Information Available

**Library of Congress Cataloging-in-Publication Data**

Rescher, Nicholas
  Sensible decisions : issues of national decision in personal choice
and public policy / Nicholas Rescher.
    p. cm.
Includes bibliographical references and index.
  ISBN 0-7425-1490-0 (cloth : alk. paper)
  1. Decision making. 2. Political planning. I. Title.
  B945.R453S46 2003
  128'.4—dc21                                    2003001014

Printed in the United States of America

⊚™ The paper used in this publication meets the minimum requirements of American
National Standard for Information Sciences—Permanence of Paper for Printed Library
Materials, ANSI/NISO Z39.48-1992.

For John Kekes,
in cordial friendship

# Contents

# Preface

In personal and public affairs alike we constantly confront the need for deciding among available alternatives. The lines of thought and principles of deliberation at issue in resolving such choices in a rationally cogent way have long preoccupied philosophers and represent an ongoing theme of theoretical scrutiny. This book is a venture at synthesizing my contribution to this discussion as it developed in my writings over many years.

Chapters 1 and 2 set the stage by surveying the setting of the issue of rational choice as a central element within the larger domain of philosophical anthropology. Here the focus is upon the rationale of rationality. Chapters 3–7 examine some key theoretical aspects of the processes of reflection through which our rational decisions are elaborated. The book then turns to matters of social decision at the public policy level. Chapters 8–11 address the situational requirements of rational procedure in the area of public issues, and consider some of the ethical or moral aspects of decision making in this domain. All in all, the book's deliberations are concerned with the procedural constraints that rationality imposes on our choices within the historical conditions of social and technological reality in which we do and must operate. Its prime aim is to illuminate some of the theoretical complications and perplexities that characterize rational procedure in matters of decision making at the public policy level.

*Part One*

# PERSONAL ISSUES

*Chapter One*

# Homo Optans:
# On the Human Condition
# and the Burden of Choice

## 1. THE UNREALIZABILITY OF PERFECTION

"Design a perfect car"; "Arrange a perfect vacation." These are instructions no one can possibly fulfill. Cars and vacations, like other goods in general, are inherently complex and subject to individuals' preferences, since it is a key fact of axiology that every evaluation-admitting object combines a *plurality* of evaluative features and every good, a plurality of desiderata. And this circumstance makes perfection unattainable. It lies in the nature of things that desirable features are, in general, competitively interactive. A conflict or competition among desiderata is an unavoidable fact of life. They cannot all be enhanced at once since more of one can only be realized at the expense of less of another. Take a car—an automobile. Here the relevant parameters of merit clearly include such factors as speed, reliability, safety, operating economy, aesthetic appearance, and road-handling ability. But in actual practice such features are interrelated. It is unavoidable that some will trade off against others. And it would be ridiculous to have a supersafe car with a maximum speed of two miles per hour or to have a car that is very inexpensive to operate but spends most of its time in a repair shop. Throughout the range of the desirable we encounter inherent conflicts among the relevant desiderata. There is no avoiding the fact that we cannot concurrently maximize all of the parameters of merit of any object of desire.

What is at issue here is something very general and very fundamental. Alike in ordinary and in philosophical usage, *perfection* is a matter of freedom from any and all limitations and deficiencies.[1] On this basis, a perfect object of some inherently valuable sort would be one that realizes every mode of relevant merit to the highest possible degree. And this is simply infeasible.

In sharpening the pencil point we render it more breakable; in enlarging the book's small print we render it more cumbersome. Every concretely realizable good is imperfect, because, as the medieval schoolmen rightly said, imperfection (*imperfectio*) is coordinate with privation (*privatio*), and the competitive interaction of desiderata means that such a shortfall in some positive respect or other is unavoidable.

This circumstance also can be regarded from another point of view. The same result is reached when perfection is viewed in Aristotle's manner that something is perfect (*teleios*) when it achieves all of its positive potentialities.[2] Taken overall, positive potentialities also will be mutually exclusive. In tightening the string of a bow or musical instrument we bring it nearer to the breaking point. And quite generally enhancing one positive potentiality can be achieved only at the cost of lessening the extent to which we can cultivate other potentialities in other directions. So in this respect, too, it transpires that perfection is unachievable.

The irony here is that the person who is intent on seeking perfection is in fact driven to immobilization. As Voltaire's dictum has it, "The best is the enemy of the good." In refusing to accept something that is less than perfect one condemns oneself to having nothing at all.

## 2. TRADE-OFFS AND OPPORTUNITY COSTS

Whenever we deal with objects of value where several concurrent desiderata are competitively involved—and thus, effectively, always—we face a situation in which synoptic, across-the-board optimization is impossible in principle because more of one value can be achieved only at the price of settling for less of another. Both uniformity and size are merits of emeralds, but an increase in one can be achieved only at the price of a decrease in the other. We want our discourse to be both pithy and adequate to the facts, but must inevitably sacrifice one to foster the other. The person who wants to be both well liked and truthful will be forced to make sacrifices one way or the other. We want the library to be both conveniently usable and comprehensive, and yet each desideratum conflicts with the other.

In pursuing objects of multidimensional value, the payment of what economists call opportunity costs becomes unavoidable. All of our efforts to obtain good objects or achieve valued objectives require us to make compromises. Throughout the domain of valued goods it transpires that some among the relevant value-constituting features can be enhanced only at the price of diminishing others.

It thus lies in the nature of things that value realization is always a matter of balance, of trade-offs, of compromise. Different aspects of merit always compete in point of realization. We can never have it both ways: a concurrent maximum in *every* dimension is simply unavailable in this or indeed any other realistically conceivable world. With inherently conflicting desiderata, across-the-board maximization is in principle impossible—in practice and generally in theory as well. All that one can ever reasonably ask for is an auspicious overall *combination* of values. Perfection—maximum realization of every value dimension all at once—is unrealizable. And it makes no sense to ask for the impossible.

## 3. THE BURDEN OF CHOICE
## AND THE INEVITABILITY OF REGRET

The unrealizability of overall perfection in the presence of competing desiderata has far-reaching consequences. It brings the inevitability of choice in its wake.

Consider a simple example. We have a housing budget of a certain fixed size. Two desiderata are foremost in our minds: (1) convenient transportation to our workplace at the center of town, and (2) spacious accommodations. In investigating the matter we find that the situation of table 1.1 prevails. At a work year of two hundred days, we can obtain additional space at the cost of one hour of additional commuting time yearly for each five square feet. We have to decide: What price (in time) are we prepared to pay for added space?

The commitment to any object of choice invariably involves such complex trade-offs among the conflicting desiderata involved. And this means that any choice is a matter of compromise—of a negotiation among those conflicting aspects of value.

All choices are accordingly a matter of closing doors, of forgoing opportunities to augment some desiderata. Every choice narrows horizons—sacrificing

**Table 1.1.  A Hypothetical Example**

| Round-trip Travel Time to and from the Town Center | Square Footage of an Accomodation Rentable on Our Budget |
|---|---|
| 0 | 1,000 |
| 0.5 hour | 1,500 |
| 1 hour | 2,000 |
| 2 hours | 3,000 |

possibilities that, in some respect, realize certain desiderata to a greater degree than we presently accept.

In such circumstances we have a situation of the inevitability of regret. Every increase in one of the relevant assets involves some loss in point of another: every gain has its dark side, invoking some sort of loss. We must acknowledge the deep and wide truth of John Gay's couplet in the *Beggar's Opera*:

> How happy could I be with either,
> Were t'other dear charmer away!

We cannot escape the exclusionary nature of choice—to opt for more of a desideratum is ipso facto to opt for less of another.

Of course, there is another side of the coin. In choosing we always sacrifice certain desiderata, but we do not do so without compensation. The sacrifices we make do—or, when we choose wisely, should—have a more than compensating return by way of benefit in respect of other desiderata. It is just that we cannot have it both ways.

Man is *Homo optans*—choosing man, a creature that must make choices. And being a rational creature as well through his status as *Homo sapiens*, this means that those choices have to be made on the basis of rationally configured evaluations. Man is thus *Homo aestimans*, evaluative man, as well. Comparative evaluation is also an unavoidable requisite of the human condition. The burden of choice—and thereby of reason-guided evaluation—is one of the definitive features of the human condition.

## 4. FINITUDE NOT AT FAULT

The reason absolute perfection is unachievable in the setting of complex goods has nothing to do with human finitude. The reason why I cannot construct a perfect house (one proximate both to my workplace and to the seashore) or build a perfect car (one that is compact for parking but roomy for passengers) has nothing to do with the limitation of my resources but lies in the inherent incompatibility of the diverse desiderata at issue.

In the more familiar range of cases we merely have a scarcity of resources—that is, we cannot spend the same dollar on each of two desired items or the same hour at two different congenial activities. In such cases we have different goods in view and cannot expend our limited resources on them all. However, in the cases now at issue, there is only a single good at stake but one that has distinct aspects of merit that are so interrelated that we cannot move several directions at once. The problem is not the scarcity of resources on *our* part but a limitation that has its roots deep in the very nature of things.

The fact that a mere augmentation of resources will not mend matters means that there is a deep irony in the condition of "the man who has everything." His affluence simply increases the range of desiderata he can satisfy individually while leaving in place the unavoidability of a conflict between those he can satisfy conjointly. He can afford to eat the greatest delicacies in unlimited quantity—but only at the expense of his health. He can afford to build his dream house and to go on his dream vacation—but immediately confronts the need to compromise by sacrificing the enjoyment of one to realize the pleasures of the other. And the difficulty here is not the limited scope of the resources of time and money and power—not human finitude—but the inherent nature of things, the natural conflict of coordinate desiderata—the fact that we cannot have our cake and eat it too, that our mechanisms can achieve greater versatility only at the cost of added complexity, and so on.

## 5. NOT MAXIMALITY BUT ACHIEVABLE OPTIMALITY

Throughout our pursuit of goods we face the choice of alternative combinations of advantages. And since we cannot pervasively *maximize,* we have to *compromise*: we have to *decide* what it is that, given our situation, is the most acceptable compromise for us. We continually confront the problem that to realize one desideratum to an acceptable extent we must assess how much are we prepared to pay in terms of the opportunity cost of a lessened realization of its competitors.

The crux is to achieve a satisfactory balance among those competing desiderata: to realize a constellation or profile of desiderata that—taken together and in combination—yields an overall result that is on balance at least as good—and certainly no worse than—any realizable alternative. The idea is a result that represents not that unrealizable ideal of "the perfect car" or "the perfect vacation," but a car or a vacation that, while obviously not *perfect*, is at least *unsurpassed* by any of the available alternatives.[3]

It is important to realize that the term *optimum* bears two quite different senses. A *strong* optimum is an alternative that is better than any other. A *weak* optimum is an alternative that is not bettered by any other—that is "as good as any to be had." Strong optima are by nature unique—there cannot be more than one. But weak optima are potentially plural and competitive.

What the preceding deliberations show is that in the pursuit of desired objects we cannot concurrently maximize with respect to all the desiderata at issue, and therefore we cannot in general hope to optimize in the strong sense of this term. There are always alternatives, and in consequence weak optimization is the best we can do. Since categorical perfection is impracticable, compromises must be made throughout the sphere of our pursuit of the good. And the choices at issue here invariably will be such that we can enhance the realization of one desideratum only at the cost of accepting the diminished realization of another.

The unattainability of perfection—the inherent impracticability of concurrently maximizing all of the modes of merit in the goods we seek—means that we are inevitably entrapped in circumstances of choice. Even as no choice in life can be made without paying an opportunity cost, so no alternative we opt for is altogether exempt from regret. This is part of what makes for what Miguel de Unamuno called the "tragic sense of life."

## NOTES

This chapter is a revised version of a paper of the same title originally published in *Idealistic Studies* 30 (2000): pp. 294–308; reprinted by kind permission of the publisher.

1. Perfection as such is absolute and idealized. To be sure there is also a subsidiary sense of the term as merely meeting the needs of a particular occasion. ("Joan is the perfect wife for John," "Tom is the perfect man for the post," "A drill is the perfect instrument for the job.") This is a different use of the term.

2. Aristotle, *Metaphysics* 16.1021b12–22a2.

3. Some writers see optimization as tantamount to maximization. (See, for example, M. A. Slote, *Beyond Optimizing* [Cambridge, Mass.: Harvard University Press, 1989].) But the present construction of the term is more faithful to its more realistic construal as addressing the best *available* rather than the best *conceivable* option.

## Chapter Two

# Why Be Rational?
# (On the Rationale of Rationality)

### 1. THE PROBLEM OF VALIDATING RATIONALITY

Why should one be rational? This may, in a way, seem to be a silly question. The answer is only too obvious—given that the rational thing to do is (effectively by definition) that for which the strongest reasons speak, we ipso facto have good reason to do it. Kurt Baier has put this point in a way difficult to improve on:

> The question "*Why* should I follow reason?" simply does not make sense. Asking it shows complete lack of understanding of the meaning of a "why question." "Why should I do this?" is a request to be given the reason for saying that I should do this. It is normally asked when someone has already said, "You should do this" and answered by giving the reason. But since "Should I follow reason?" means "Tell me whether doing what is supported by the best reasons is doing what is supported by the best reasons," there is simply no possibility of adding "Why?" For the question now comes to this, "Tell me the reason why doing what is supported by the best reasons is doing what is supported by the best reasons." It is exactly like asking, "Why is a circle a circle?"[1]

In virtue of its nature as such, the rational resolution to an issue is the best solution we can manage—the one that we *should* adopt and *would* adopt if we were to proceed intelligently. The impetus to rationality is grounded in our commitment to proceeding intelligently—to "using our brains." ("Why be rational?" "It's the intelligent thing to do." "But why proceed intelligently?" "Come now; surely you jest!") After all, once we admit that something is the best thing to do, what *further* reason could we possibly want for doing it? Once it is settled that *A* is the rational thing to do—which may itself take a lot of showing—there is no more room for any *further* reason for doing *A*, no

further point to asking "Why do *A*?" For *at this stage*, the best of reasons—
by *hypothesis*—already speak for doing *A*. Once rationality is established,
there are no further extra- (or supra-) rational reasons to which we could sensibly appeal for validation. In this sense, then, the question "Why do the rational thing?" is simply foolish: it is a request for further reasons at a juncture
at which, by hypothesis, all the needed reasons are already in.

But this line of response to our question, though perfectly cogent, is a bit too
facile. The job that needs to be accomplished is actually more complicated.

Belief, action, and evaluation based on what really are—truly and actually—
the "best of reasons" must necessarily be successful. This contention is simply
circular, since those theoretically best of reasons are best exactly because they
ensure realization of the best results. But, in this world, we are not in general in
a position to proceed from the actual best as such, but only from the visible best
that is at our disposal—"the best *available* (or *discernible*) reasons." We have
to content ourselves with doing "the *apparently* best thing"—the best that is determinable in the prevailing circumstances. But the fact remains that the alternatives whose adoption we ourselves sensibly and appropriately view as rational given the information at our disposal at the time are not necessarily
*actually* optimal. The problem with doing the rational thing—doing what we
sensibly suppose to be supported by the best reasons—is that our information,
being incomplete, may well point us in the wrong direction. Facing this
"predicament of reason," we know the pitfalls, realizing full well the fragility
of these best laid schemes. So the problem remains: Why should we act on the
most promising visible alternative, when visibility is restricted to the limited
horizons of our own potentially inadequate vantage point whose potential inadequacy we cannot but acknowledge?

In answering this question, let us begin by considering the situation in light
of the expected-value calculation set out in table 2.1. It is clear in the context
there postulated that as long as *d*, the increment in the probability of success due
to heeding rationality's advice, is greater than zero—that is, as long as doing the
rationally advisable thing will increase the probability of success somewhat, no
matter how little—then this course is the decision-theoretically sensible one. As
long as rationality improves the prospects of success, no matter how modestly,
its call represents the best bet, the advisable course, the sensible thing to do. No
*guarantees* are necessary.

After all, in this imperfect sublunary dispensation, probability is, as Bishop
Butler said, "the guide of life." We must—*rationally* must—follow the guidance of the perceived probability that the general policy of doing the rationally indicated thing will, on balance and over time, prove to be our best bet.
Rationality is not a thing of the present moment and the case in hand, but of
the whole picture and the long run.

**Table 2.1. Rationality in Decision-Theoretic Perspective**

| | I Do Not Do the Rationally Advisable Thing | I Do the Rationally Advisable Thing |
|---|---|---|
| Probability of achieving (optimal) success | $p$ | $p + d$ |
| Probability of failing to achieve (optimal) success | $1 - p$ | $1 - (p + d)$ |
| Value of achieving (optimal) success | $x$ | $x$ |
| Value of failing to achieve (optimal) success | $y$ | $y$ |

The following expected values emerge:

$$EV \text{ (non-rat'1)} = px + (1 - p)y = p(x - y) + y$$

$$EV \text{ (rat'1)} = (p + d)x + (1 - p - d)y = p(x - y) + d(x - y) + y$$

*Note*: EV(rat'1) > EV(non- rat'1) iff $d(x - y) > 0$ iff $d > 0$ (since obviously $(x - y) > 0$).

The rational person is, by definition, someone who uses intelligence to maximize the probability—that is, the *responsibly formed subjective probability*— that matters will eventuate favorably for the promotion of his real interests. It is just this that makes following the path of rationality the rational course. Rationality calls for adopting the overall best (visible) alternative—the best that is, in practice, available to us in the circumstances. And if *A* indeed is the rational thing to do in this sense, then we should expect to be worse off in doing something different from *A*. To be sure, things may not come to that; we could be lucky. But this is something we have not earned and certainly have no grounds to expect.

After all, why do we endorse the world descriptions of the science of the day? Why do we follow the medical recommendations of the physicians of the day, or the policy recommendations of the economists of the day? Because we know them to be correct—or at any rate highly likely to be true? Not at all! We know or believe no such thing—historical experience is too strongly counterindicative. Rather, we accept them as guides only because we see them as more promising than any of the *identifiable* alternatives that we are in a position to envision. We accept them because they afford us the greatest available subjective probability of success—discernibly the best bet.

We do not proceed with unalloyed confidence, but rather with the resigned recognition that we can do no better at the moment. Similarly, the recommendations of reason afford not a guarantee of success, but merely the *best overall chances* of reaching our goals. We act, in short, on the basis of faute de mieux considerations, of this or nothing better—"as far as the eye reaches." In real-world situations reason trades in courses of action whose efficacy is a matter of hope and whose rationalization is a matter of this-or-nothing-better argumentation.

Like the drowning man, we clutch at the best available object. We recognize full well that even the most rationally laid scheme can misfire. Reality is not always and inevitably on the side of the strongest arguments. Reason affords no guarantee of success, but only the reassurance that one has made the best rational bet—of having done as well as one could in the circumstances of the case. One cannot say, flatly and unqualifiedly: "You should be rational because rationality pays in rendering success if not certain then at any rate more probable." Rather, we have to content ourselves with: "You should be rational because this affords the best rationally foreseeable prospects of success—on the whole and in the long run." And while we live in the partial and limited short run, rationality affords our best prospect of going further. And of course in the larger scheme of things, experience itself informs us about those issues where the best we can do is good enough and those where it is not.[2]

However, with all this said and done, the problem of real or objective versus apparent or subjective optimality that was our starting point remains in place. This whole approach turns on the supposition that "doing the rational thing" will indeed enhance our overall chances of bringing our affairs to a successful issue. Is this actually true?

To all appearances, the answer is a resounding "of course!" What is at issue here is seemingly a tautology. Clearly, if that object did not have a blade, we would not call it a "knife." Equally clearly, if we did not accept that doing *A* would enhance the chances of the relevant sort of success, then we would not characterize *A* as "the rational thing to do in the circumstances." We simply could not endorse that course of action as being rationally advisable in the circumstances if we were not convinced that it enhanced the chances of a successful issue. It is just this that makes something into the "rational thing to do": its enhancing, as best we can tell, our chances of attaining success to a greater extent than any other available alternative. We may have trouble spotting the rational thing to do in particular circumstances, but once our minds are made up about this, then the issue of rational advisability is closed.

Unfortunately, however, this is still not quite the end of it. The problem remains: Just exactly what are the probabilities with which we are operating? Of course, we *intend* them to be objective, real-world likelihoods; this is what we would ideally *like* to have. But, in fact, of course, they are no more than our considered *estimates* of such likelihoods as best we can shape them in the light of the available information. And this means that we are once again in the presence of rational resolutions effected on the basis of the *available* data. We are here confronted with an instant, local replay of the global problem that is being addressed. Striving to escape the predicament of reason, it mocks us by leaping ahead to bar our way. We here confront once more the familiar and vexing issue of the actual optimality of apparent optima. And there is nothing we can do to escape this awkward circumstance—we simply have to take it in our stride.

The fact of the matter is that we cannot prove that rationality pays—necessarily, or even only probabilistically, in the long run. We do not know that acting rationally in the particular case at hand will *actually* pay off—nor can we even claim with unalloyed assurance that it will *probably* do so (with real likelihood rather than subjective probability). We can only say that, as best we can judge the matter, it represents the most promising course at our disposal. We have no guarantees—no means are at our disposal for preestablishing that following rationality's counsel actually pays.

Consider the sequence of theses that, by doing the rational thing in the present case, we shall, *as best we can tell*:

1. ensure ourselves success;
2. ensure ourselves success if success is at all possible;
3. enhance the chances of success (its objective probability) in this present case;
4. enhance the chances of a good record of success overall in the whole series of similar cases.

As we move down this list, we reach increasingly weaker and thus more plausible contentions. To achieve something tenable we must go all the way down to the bottom of the list at item four. And even here we must settle for the *visible* as opposed to *real* chances. The efficacy of rationality can be maintained only in the qualified way of a reasonable expectation. Throughout our cognitive and practical affairs we have to conduct our operations under conditions of risk.

## 2. THE PRAGMATIC TURN: EVEN COGNITIVE RATIONALITY HAS A PRAGMATIC BASIS

No considerations of theoretical, general principle can possibly establish that what is *apparently* the optimal course—what is so as best one can tell—is *actually* optimal. In this matter we cannot proceed by way of cogent inference in the evidential/cognitive order of reason, but must turn in another direction altogether, to inference in the *practical* order of reason. The best available justification of rationality is a practical inference along the following lines:

1. We want and need rationally cogent answers to our questions—answers that optimally reflect the available information.
2. Following the path of cognitive rationality (as standardly construed) is the best *available* way to secure rationally cogent answers to our questions.

*Therefore*: Following the path of standard cognitive rationality in matters of inquiry (that is, in answering our questions) is the rational thing to do: we are rationally well advised to answer our questions in line with the standard processes of cognitive rationality.

It must be stressed that this reasoning is of the following pattern: We have the inherently appropriate objective $O$; course of action $A$ is the optimal available path to this objective; therefore, we are rationally well advised to follow this path. This, clearly, is a quintessentially pragmatic style of argumentation.

It is appropriate to proceed rationally not because we know that by so doing we will (inevitably or probably) succeed, but because we realize that by doing so we will have done the very best we possibly can toward producing this outcome: we will have given the matter our best shot.[3]

This practical turn is ultimately inevitable. We can do no more than to adopt an approach that represents the best and the most that we can do. Of course we cannot maintain: "If you form a belief rationally, then it will turn out to be true." This is simply not in the cards. The most we can do is to maintain: "By all the relevant indications, there is good reason to think that a rationally formed belief is true. (That is exactly what we *mean* by 'a rationally formed belief.')" The cogency of our practical argument rests on the fact that in real-life situations we simply have to do the best we can—that it would be senseless (and irrational!) to ask for more than this.

To summarize, the answer to our pivotal question—"Why do the normatively *rational* thing, given that we cannot guarantee its success?"—lies in a confluence of considerations:

1. As far as we can tell, it is the best thing to do (it is the *apparent* optimum).
2. While *apparent* optima are not necessarily *real* optima—are not necessarily optimal as such—experience teaches that we cannot find a policy superior to that of doing what is apparently optimal. ("This or nothing better.")

3. By adopting this policy (on "win or lose, it is the best we can do" grounds), we most effectively subserve the crucial desideratum of ensuring we have done the very best that is possible for us in the circumstances.

And the reason why we rest content with such a practical argument itself proceeds in the practical mode:

1. We have a certain (appropriate) objective—namely, to ensure legitimacy and interpersonal efficacy of coordination essential to successful collaborative action.
2. We recognize that practical reason affords our only really practicable way to obtain such coordination and validation. ("This or nothing.")

*Therefore*: We are rationally well advised to adopt the way of practical reason in validating reason.

The sort of argument for rationality that we have contemplated is thus a *practical* argument rather than one that proceeds in the strictly cognitive sector of reason. And this is the best that can be had. To decline it—to say that the best available is simply not good enough—is simply to be irrational. Not surprisingly, rationality here stands on the side of reason.

Philosophers of pragmatic inclination have always stressed the ultimate inadequacy of any strictly theoretical defense of cognitive rationality. And their instincts in this regard are surely right. One cannot marshal an ultimately satisfactory defense of rational cognition by an appeal that proceeds *wholly* on its own grounds. In providing a viable justification the time must come for stepping outside the whole cognitive/theoretical sphere and seeking for some extracognitive support for our cognitive proceedings. It is at just this stage that a *pragmatic* appeal to the condition of effective action properly comes into operation.

And this pragmatic aspect of the matter has yet another side. The pivotal role of rationality as a coordination principle also must be emphasized. Adequate cultivation of our individual interest requires a coordination of effort with others and imposes the need for cooperation and collaboration.[4] But this is achievable only if we "understand" one another. And here rationality becomes critical. It is a crucial resource for mutual understanding, for rendering people comprehensible to one another, so as to make effective communication and cooperation possible.

The following three points are crucial in this regard: (1) It is a matter of life and death for us to live in a setting where we ourselves are in large measure predictable for others, because only on this basis of mutual predictability can we achieve conditions essential to our own welfare. (2) The easiest way to become predictable for others is to act in such a way that they can explain, understand, and anticipate my actions on the basis of the question "What would I do if I were in his shoes?" (3) In this regard, the "apparent best" is the obvious choice, not only because of its (admittedly loose) linkage to optimality per se, but also because of its "*saliency*." The quest for "the best available" leads one to fix on that alternative at which others, too, could be expected to arrive in the circumstances—so that they can also understand one's choices.

The pursuit of optimality is accordingly a determinative factor for rationality not only through its direct benefits in yielding our best apparent chances of success, but also through its providing a principle for the guidance of action that achieves the crucial requisite of social coordination in the most efficient realizable way. (But why coordinate on what is *rational*? Why not simply coordinate on habit or fashion or "the done thing"? Partly, because these leave us in the lurch once we get off the beaten track of the usual course of things. And partly because they are unstable and inherently unreliable.)

### 3. THE SELF-RELIANCE OF RATIONALITY IS NOT VICIOUSLY CIRCULAR

This practical line of argumentation may still seem to leave the situation in an unsatisfactory state. It says (roughly): "You should be rational in resolving your choices because *it is rational to believe that* the best available prospects of optimality attainment are effectively realized in this way." To be sure, one might deem it preferable if that italicized clause were wholly suppressed. A skeptic is bound to press the following objection: The proposed practicalistic legitimation of reason conforms to the pattern: "You should be rational just because that is the rational thing to do!" And this is clearly circular.

It might seem questionable to establish the jurisdiction of reason by appeal to the judgment of reason itself. But, in fact, this circularity is not really vicious at all. Vicious circularity stultifies by "begging the question"; virtuous circularity merely coordinates related elements in their mutual interlinkage. The former presupposes what is to be proved; the latter simply shows how things are connected in a well-coordinated and mutually supportive interrelationship. The self-reliance of rationality merely exemplifies this latter circumstance of an inherent coordination among its universe components.

Admittedly, the reasoning at issue has an *appearance* of vitiating circularity because the force of the argument itself rests on an appeal to rationality: "If you are going to be rational in your beliefs, then you must also act rationally, because it is rational to believe that rational action is optimal in point of goal attainment." But this sort of question begging is simply *unavoidable* in the circumstances. It is exactly what we want and need. Where else should we look for a *rational* validation of rationality but to reason itself? The only reasons for being rational that it makes sense to ask for are *rational* reasons. In this epistemic dispensation, we have no way of getting at the facts directly, without the epistemic detour of securing grounds and reasons for them. And it is, of course, rationally cogent grounds and reasons that we want and need. The overall justification of rationality *must* be reflexive and self-referential. To provide a rationale of rationality is to show that rationality stands in appropriate alignment with the principles of rationality. From the angle of justification, rationality is a cyclic process that closes in on itself, not a linear process that ultimately rests on something outside itself.

There is accordingly no basis for any rational discontent, no room for any dissatisfaction or complaint regarding a "circular" justification of rationality. We would not (should not) want it otherwise. If we bother to want an answer to the question "Why be rational?" at all, it is clearly a *rational* answer that we require. The only sort of justification of anything—rationality included—that is worth having is a rational one. That presupposition of rationality is not vitiating, not viciously circular, but essential—an unavoidable consequence of the self-sufficiency of cognitive reason. There is simply no satisfactory alternative to using reason in its own defense. Already embarked on the sea of rationality, we want such assurance as can now be made available that we have done the right thing. And such reassurance can indeed be given—exactly along the lines just indicated. Given the very nature of the justificatory enterprise at issue, one just cannot avoid letting rationality sit in judgment on itself. (What is being asked for, after all, is a rational argument for rational action, a basis for rational conviction, and not persuasion by something probatively irrelevant such as threats of force majeure.) One would expect, nay *demand*, that rationality be self-substantiating in this way—that it *must* emerge as the best policy on its own telling.

From the justificatory point of view, rationality is and must be autonomous. It can be subject to no external authority. Rationality in general is a matter of systematization, and the justification of rationality is correspondingly a matter of systemic self-sufficiency. Rather than indicating the defect of vicious circularity, the self-referential character of a justification of rationality is a precondition of its adequacy! It is *only* a rational legitimation of rationality that we would want: any other sort would avail us nothing. And if such a rational validation were not forthcoming, this would indicate a grave defect.

To be sure, some theorists see rationality as heteronomous—as subject to some external sort of authority such as "feeling" or "the will." Thus, one contemporary philosopher projects the idea that:

> [U]nderlying each . . . judgment there is a choice that the agent has made—a type of choice in which the individual is at the most fundamental level unconstrained by good reasons, precisely because his or her choice expresses a decision as to what is to count as a good reason for him or her.[5]

Such a view sees rational justification as linear and regressive—and thus as ultimately having to rest on an unrationalized rock bottom that itself lies quite outside the domain of reason. But any such view is profoundly mistaken. Rational validation is not linear and regressive, but rather cyclical and systemically self-contained. We need not—must not—subscribe to the rock-bottom fallacy. There is no way of grounding good reasons in arbitrary or otherwise unrationalizable decisions. ("Deciding as to what is to count as a good reason" forsooth! Not even God is in a position to do that!)[6] No one *decides* what sorts of things are to count as good reasons. In general, we only learn in the school of experience what qualifies as such.

A certain irrationalism is astir in the world that rejects the quest for rationally validated reasons and advocates a freewheeling "anything goes"—even in the cognitive sphere of empirical inquiry.[7] But, of course, any sensible person not already committed to such a position would want to know if there is any good reason for taking it. And then we are at once back in the sphere of rationality and good reasons.

Thus, the predicament of reason gives no comfort to skepticism or irrationalism and yields no grounds for abandoning reason or, worse yet, for turning against her. This self-supportive legitimation of rationality is the only cogent sort of validation that we are going to get. But, in the final analysis, it is the only sort that it makes sense to ask for, seeing that rationality itself enjoins us to view the best we can possibly get as good enough.[8]

Yet, does reason's self-reliance not open the door to skepticism? Skeptics have always insisted on just this point that we cannot *prove* in advance of conceding reason's cogency that we will not go wrong by trusting our reason. And this—so we have granted—is quite correct. But, of course, what one can do is to establish that if we reject reason, we cut ourselves off from any (rationally warranted) expectation of success. There are no guarantees that our ventures in trust are going to prove successful; whether our trust is actually warranted in any given circumstances (trust in ourselves, in our cognitive faculties, in other people, and the like) is something we cannot in the nature of things ascertain in advance of events. A conjunction of trust with hope and faith is germane alike to the cognitive project, the practical project, and the evaluative project. Throughout, we have to conduct our operations under conditions of risk, without confidence in outcomes and without advance guarantees of success. In all these matters efficacy is a matter of hope and confidence in the best available option whose rationalization is a matter of this-or-nothing-better argumentation.

Such argumentation will not of course satisfy the skeptic. For him, the lack of guarantees undermines the whole project of rationality. The skeptic's objections to cognitive rationality deserve the fuller treatment of a separate chapter.

## 4. WHY BE RATIONAL?

Reason requires that we do what is appropriate in matters of belief, evaluation, and action—that we use our intelligence to figure out the proper thing to do and then do it. But why should we do what reason demands? Why heed the demands of reason?

Note this is *not* asking for a validation of reason from without. There can be no such thing. The only sort of validation of anything—reason included—that is worth having is a reasonable one. The validation of rationality is a matter of asking exactly what rationality can say on its own behalf.

One may of course quite appropriately ask questions such as: Why be rational? Why should I cultivate the truth? Why should I cultivate my best (or true) interests? But in the very act of posing these questions I am asking for reasons—that is, I am evincing my commitment to the project of rationality. Caring for the truth and for one's best interests are simply part and parcel of this commitment. If I do not care for these things, then there is really no point in raising these questions. In this event I have *already* taken my place outside the precincts of rationality, beyond the reach of reason. From the justificatory point of view, rationality is and must be autonomous. It can be subject to no external authority. Cognitive rationality in general is a matter of harmonious systematization, and the justification of rationality is correspondingly a matter of systemic self-sufficiency. At this point there is little more to be said. If I want a reason at all, I must want a *rational* reason. If I care about reasons at all, I am already within the project of rationality. But once I am *within* the project, there is nothing *further* external to reason that can *or need* be said to validate it. At *that* stage rationality is already at hand to provide its own support—it wears its justification on its sleeve. (The project of trying to reason with someone who stands *outside* the range of rationality to convince them to come into its fold is clearly an exercise in pointlessness and futility.)

Irrationality—wishful thinking and self-deception—may be convenient and even, in some degree, psychologically comforting. But it is neither cognitively nor reflectively satisfactory. If it is a viable defense of a position that we want, it is bound to be a rational one. The only validation of rationality that can reasonably be asked for—and the only one worth having—must lie in considerations of the systemic self-sufficiency of reason. In the final analysis, "Why be rational?" must be answered with the only rationally appropriate response: "Because rationality itself obliges us to be so." In providing a *rational* justification of rationality—and what other kind would we want?—the best we can do is to follow the essentially circular (but *nonviciously* circular!) line of establishing that reason herself endorses taking this course. Reason's self-recommendation is an important *and necessary* aspect of the legitimation of this enterprise. But how is one to proceed in rationally justifying rationality? The only and appropriate way is through the consideration that rationality is in its very nature teleological and ends oriented. Cognitive rationality is concerned with achieving true beliefs. Evaluative rationality is concerned with making correct evaluations. Practical rationality is concerned with the effective pursuit of appropriate objectives. Rationality being a teleological enterprise, its validation does and must proceed in a pragmatic manner with reference to purposive efficacy. It pivots on the question of effectiveness in the context of given ends: of benefits and costs if you will.

What do we stand to lose by going against the demands of reason? Here the matter stands as follows: In ignoring (let alone violating)

| *cognitive* ⎫ | | accepting falsehoods |
|---|---|---|
| *evaluative* ⎬ rationality we run an | ⎰ endorsing inferior items |
| *practical* ⎭ avoidable risk of | ⎱ failing to achieve appropriate ends |

In each case we are dealing with an enterprise that has objectives. And in failing to heed the standards at issue we are in each case putting the achievement of these objectives at risk. Accordingly, the *validation of rationality consists in the consideration that its violation would compromise the successful pursuit of appropriate ends*. And this argumentation is itself a paradigm of a pragmatic/teleological validation.

Note that all of rationality is engaged in this process of validating reason. It pivots on there being (cognitively) sound reason to think that an (evaluatively) appropriate end of the enterprise will become less likely to be (practically) realized. We have here a line of deliberation in which all of the sectors of rationality are at work. But in its overall nature the justification is *pragmatic* by way of pivoting on the issue of purpose realization.

And there is good reason for this pragmatic orientation. How is one to refute those who set rationality at naught? How can we argue against the skeptical nihilist who refuses to accept any and all truth claims or the psychopath who has a totally weird system of values and priorities or the madman whose actions deliberately frustrate the realization of his own ends?

Take the skeptic who rejects all of the usual ground rules of epistemic practice and refuses to accept anything whatsoever. How can one possibly *reason* against him—argue him out of his position. All rational argumentation proceeds from premises, from something accepted (at least pro tem). One who rejects everything—accepts nothing—obviously allows no fulcrum for the lever of reasoning.

Or, take the nihilist who rejects all the usual values that people hold or the psychopath who persists in setting the value of other people and their interests at naught. Such a person is beyond the reach of moral deliberation because matters in this domain can only be addressed *rationally* on the basis of standards—that is, by proceeding from an evaluative standpoint vis-à-vis personhood. The values nihilist clearly places himself outside the reach of rational appeal and moral suasion.

Again, take the madman whose actions frustrate his own aims. His failure is not—or need not be—one of logical reasoning. At each step of a dialectic of argumentation he would well come up with some weird story to rationalize his actions.

We have no alternative but to acknowledge that we cannot refute such rationality rejectors by *purely* logico-theoretical reasoning. Those who turn their backs on the principles of reason are for this very reason secure from defeat by reason's means. We will then be unable as a matter of course to secure a foothold for logico-theoretical argumentation to get under way.

In opposing nihilism in its various forms we have to proceed in the mode of practical rather than logico-theoretical reason. The "inconsistency" in which these people are caught up lies in this practical rather than theoretical domain. The crux is that in abandoning rationality we discernably compromise the chances of accomplishing our own ends—those to which we commit ourselves upon entering into the theoretical and practical projects at issue.

We cannot reasonably set it up as a task for the rational enterprise to discharge the in-principle impossible mission of convincing an (otherwise rational) moral nihilist (psychopath) to walk in the paths of morality and benevolence. Nor does it make sense to ask for argumentation to convince an (otherwise rational) epistemic nihilist (skeptic) to walk in the paths of ordinary rational inquiry. In all such cases, the aim of the enterprise must be conceived of as involving no more (though also no less) than convincing otherwise rational and normal (commonsensical) people that they should not become psychopaths or skeptics in the first place. Striving for more exacts costs that yield no compensating benefits. It suffices to show that from the angle of such (normal, commonsensical) people as we generally find in the world about us there is no suitable balance of advantages gained over benefit forgone in being skeptical or psychopathic.

And this task is not all that difficult. The skeptic says, "I have such high epistemic standards that nothing can meet them." But what does this gain him? Nothing: he leaves the cognitive playing field altogether empty-handed with all questions unanswered. The psychopath says, "I set the value of others and their interests at naught." Now this does indeed gain him *something*, namely, the advantage of not having to bother about others. But it gives this advantage at the expense of the resulting isolation and loss of bonds of affection and congeniality that exact a horrendous price in terms of alienation and misery—at any rate, for normal people.

In the only way in which it makes sense to be concerned about the question "Why be rational?" then, there is a perfectly good and satisfactory response. It makes sense in the manner of all practical reasoning, to wit, that failing to do this produces significant losses not compensated for by preponderating benefits. Rationality has the perfectly rational justification that in failing to heed the dictates of reason we came up on the short end of the balance of benefits gained versus advantages forgone.

The aim of the enterprise of grappling with the question "Why be rational?" is not, however, to refute the skeptic or refute the psychopath by some categorical demonstration that this position is logically untenable, unavoidable to any rational person who is prepared to maintain the position come what may and simply accept whatever negativities this involves. Rather, the aim is to point out that taking this position calls for paying a price that *sensible* people (*l'homme moyen rational*) would be unwilling to pay because the cost/benefit, gain/loss balance stands too adversely. We accept the guidance of reason because rational considerations indicate that this affords us the *best overall chances* of reaching our goals. We act, in short, on the basis of faute de mieux considerations, of "this or nothing better—as far as the eye reaches."

The fact of the matter is that we cannot *prove* that rationality pays. All that we know is that being rational in the case at hand is the (rationally) best we can do in the circumstances.[9] We recognize full well that even the most rationally laid scheme can misfire. Reality is not always and inevitably on the side of the strongest arguments. And in any case, we see into the future but dimly. Reason affords no guarantee of success, but only the assurance of having made the best rational bet—of having done as well as one could in the circumstances of the case. One cannot say, flatly and unqualifiedly: "You should be rational because rationality pays in rendering success if not certain then at any rate more probable." Rather, we have to content ourselves with: "You should be rational because this affords the best rationally foreseeable prospects of success—on the whole and in the long run."

And so, we follow reason because it makes good rational sense to do so, seeing that it affords us with the best visible prospect for realizing our objectives. One should be rational in general for just the same sort of reason as the hungry man should be rational in choosing to eat bread over sand—namely, that by all available indications this course represents the most promising prospect of attaining one's sensible goals.[10]

Throughout our cognitive and practical affairs we have to conduct our operations under conditions of risk. And so, when we do the rational thing but it just does not pan out, we simply have to grin and bear it. The matter is one of calculated risks and plausibly expectable benefits. Rationality affords no guarantees. By the very nature of what is involved in rational procedure, the determinable odds are in its favor. But that may still be cold comfort when things go wrong. Then, all we have is the satisfaction of having done our best. The long and short of the matter is that nothing obliges us to be rational except our rationality itself.

Of course, one may somehow *prefer* not to be rational. With belief, I may prefer congeniality to truth. With action, I may prefer convenience to optimality. With value, I may prefer the pleasingly base to the more austere better. On all sides, I may willfully opt for what I simply like, rather than for what is normatively appropriate. But if I do this, I lose sight of the actual ends of the cognitive, practical, and evaluative enterprises, to the detriment of my *real* (as opposed to *apparent*) interests. It lies in the nature of things that reason is on the side of rationality. To be sure, she offers us no guarantees. Yet, if we abandon reason, there is no place better that we can (rationally) go.

## NOTES

1. Kurt Baier, *The Moral Point of View,* abridged ed. (New York: Random House, 1965), pp. 160–61.

2. Compare Herbert Simon, *Models of Bounded Rationality*, 3 vols. (Cambridge, Mass.: MIT Press, 1997).

3. In his interesting book *A Justification of Rationality* (Albany: State University of New York Press, 1976), John Kekes argues that "the justification of rationality is . . . [as] a device for problem-solving and it should be employed because everybody has problems, because it is in everybody's interest to solve his problems, and because rationality is the most promising way of doing so" (p. 168). This traditionally pragmatic view is very

close to our own position except that it pivots rationality's justification on effectiveness in problem solving, while our position is somewhat more cautious. It does not contend that the course of reason actually is our best recourse in problem solving, but only that it is so as best we can (rationally) judge. The present argumentation thus brings the aspect of reason's self-reliance to the fore as a critical aspect of the justification of rationality, and accordingly is not a pure pragmatism.

4. On this theme see R. Axelrod and W. D. Hamilton, "The Evolution of Cooperation," *Science* 211 (1981): pp. 1390–96.

5. Alasdair MacIntyre, in *Revisions,* ed. MacIntyre and Stanley Haverwas (Notre Dame and London: Notre Dame University Press, 1983), p. 9.

6. On this point, see Leibniz's correspondence with Arnauld regarding the *Discourse on Metaphysics*.

7. See, e.g., Paul K. Feyerabend, *Against Method* (London and New York: Humanities Press, 1978).

8. *Est ridiculum quaerere quae habere non possumus*, as Cicero wisely observed (*Pro Archia*, iv. 8).

9. Aspects of this theme are also discussed in the author's *Rationality* (Oxford: Clarendon Press, 1988).

10. Compare René Descartes, *Discourse on Method*, sect. iii, maxim 2.

## Chapter 3

# Is Reasoning about Values
# Viciously Circular?

Can value judgments be rationally validated without vicious, or at least vitiating, circularity? In addressing this question it helps to begin with an analogy by asking this same question about substantive facts rather than normative values.

Suppose that we have some modes of fact-substantive argumentation at our disposal: $A_1, A_2, \ldots, A_n$. Let it be that our assigned task is to justify their use—to validate them, in short, by some process of reasoning. To validate $A_1$ we must, of course, use some argumentation. If circular reasoning is proscribed and self-employment accordingly prohibited, then we can use only some of the remaining $A_i$ here. To this end we have at most $n - 1$ modes of argumentation at our disposal. For the sake of convenience, let it be that $A_2$ is one of them. But now let us ask about the validation of $A_2$. Both $A_2$ itself and $A_1$ are now ineligible on grounds of circularity. We thus have at most $n - 2$ arguments at our disposal for validating $A_2$. And now the handwriting is on the wall. By the time it comes down to validating $A_n$, we will thus have at most $n - n = 0$ modes of argumentation at our disposal. There is now *nothing* to be done. The lesson is crystal clear. If circularity is altogether proscribed in the regressive validation of modes of substantiative argument—if a given mode of argumentation is never to be used, directly or indirectly, in the course of its own validation—then it will be impossible to validate the entire manifold of arguments that we employ.

To be sure, there is one seeming exception here. The preceding line of reasoning supposes, naturally enough, that the manifold of argumentation modes at issue will be finite. Clearly, if this were not so, and if the argumentation modes at our disposal were an endless series, $A_1, A_2, A_3, \ldots$, then *every* argument mode could be validated in terms of others yet further down the line. Circularity—direct or indirect—could now readily be averted. But of course this is a process that we could never actually carry out. The project of validating the entire spectrum of our modes of argumentation, which, after all, was the aim of the enterprise, is now a lost cause from the outset and validation becomes a Sisyphus-like project that one could always pursue but never complete. After all, we are finite creatures that have only limited resources of time and information at our disposal. To be of effective use to us, the processes of validation must come to an end—they too must be finite. In this justificatory context a process that we cannot bring to a successful conclusion is a process that cannot achieve its goal.

This line of thought goes to show that we cannot forgo the circularity of self-involvement in the context of validating the modes of supportive argumentation that we use in substantiating our factual claims. In various other contexts of reasoning, such as demonstration and explanation, circularity may well be vicious and vitiating. But in the realm of argument validation it is inevitable and indispensable.

As with facts so it is with values. The processes at issue with cognitive regress breed true to type as it were, even as a correct definition of a musical or archeological term must involve musical or archeological conceptions. In particular, it is a pivotal epistemic principle that both in demonstrative and in non-demonstrative inference a cogent cognitive regress must be thematically homogeneous: the clarifying or justifying account for a claim must always incorporate at least some commitments of the same thematic type as those at issue in the claim itself. Thus, a cogent reason for a factual claim must itself be factual in the sense of involving at least some factual commitments, and exactly the same is true of evaluative and practical claims. Such cognitive regresses stay within the same topical arena: a cognitive item's regressive antecedents must always be of the same basic type as the item itself.

What is at issue here is nothing vicious but the mere operation of the ex nihilo nihil principle. If we want to conduct a course of reasoning that validates facts we must use facts by way of input—and the situation with respect to values (or for that matter obligation or desiderata) is just the same.

To be sure, the situation comes to be different when we turn from cognitive to noncognitive regresses such as causation. Causal production is by no means thematically homogeneous: life can come from nonlife, liquid from nonliquid. But with cognitive regresses, there is no such thing as an origin of species; things have to run true to type across the successive regressive stages. Thus, rationality is in this regard decisively different from causality, where, as Darwin taught, new species can readily emerge. In matters of cognitive substantiation the filiation of thematic connection between contention and reason must always be preserved. In the cognitive realm, unlike the physical, the ancient Greek principle that "like can only come from like" obtains.

It should be noted that rational evaluation is also a form of cognition, seeing that what is at issue is simply knowledge about matters of value rather than about matters of fact. So here too justification is subject to what might be called the principle of thematic homogeneity. Evaluative conclusions can be substantiated only via premises that are somewhere along the line evaluative in their substance. Even as factual theses can be substantiated only through premises of which at least some are of a factual character, so evaluative conclusions are substantiable only by means of premises some of which are of a evaluative nature.

The thematic homogeneity means that substantiative arguments to evaluative conclusions must have evaluative inputs. The crucial point is that the value realm is inferentially closed. One cannot enter it inferentially from without. To provide a discursive or inferential validation of an evaluative conclusion, one must have recourse to at least some evaluative inputs as premises for the reasoning, even if only in inherently trivial cases. Inferentially, values must root in values: where *only* ostensibly value-free facts go in, values cannot come out.

Is such thematic homogeneity something vicious or vitiating where values are concerned? By no means. Here the following considerations come into play.

There is, indeed, an important difference between factual and evaluative substantiation, which can be brought to light as follows. The circumstance that one must always use some facts to substantiate facts does not lead to circularity because you can in principle always use *different* facts, seeing as the factual domain is not finite (if only because there are also mathematical facts). However, we must also use values to substantiate values. And the evaluative domain is finite since the value spectrum, though large, is nevertheless limited. So here the situation is substantially analogous to the thesis "You must use arguments to validate arguments," which was discussed at the outset. In consequence, value validation like argument validation is in a way self-involving: we must use objects of the sort at issue in the course of validating such objects. So here too there will be a circularity of sorts since the regress must come to a stop. But we arrive here at the instructive conclusion that in such situations of thematic homogeneity, circular, or at any rate cyclic, reasoning becomes inescapable. The sort of circularity at issue with thematic homogeneity is not a matter of viciousness but rather of rational cogency, seeing that in these cognitive contexts the principle ex nihilo nihil obtains.

Another important consideration also comes into play here. The value involvement of evaluative demonstration does not actually vitiate the discursive validation of our value judgments because while evaluative inputs are unavoidable, they are also in the end trivial. While it is indeed true that the fact–value divide cannot be crossed by cogent demonstration without using some evaluative premises, at least tacitly, it nevertheless can be crossed when the premises are trivial and truistic. For example, consider the inference:

Doing *A* would cause Smith needless and pointless distress.
*Therefore*: It would be wrong for me, or anyone, to do A.

To be sure, this perfectly valid inference is only enthymematically so. To achieve demonstrative stringency we must have recourse to the enthymematic premise: "It is wrong to do something that avoidably causes people needless and pointless pain." But this premise is unproblematically available. It is, in fact, close to trivial since the mode of action at issue is a paradigm instance of moral transgression: given that pain is clearly something negative for us, its pointless and unnecessary infliction on some of us by others is a quintessential malfeasance.[1]

The salient consideration is that values *almost* emerge from facts—that the gap between facts and values, while important, is nevertheless often such a small one that it can be crossed by a step so short as to be effectively trivial, namely, by means of truisms of the sort at issue with the negativity of inflicting *needless* pain.

The salient fact is that in innumerable situations, the transition from factual premises to evaluative conclusions is mediated by frequently enthymematic evaluative premises that are essentially trivial and truistic in that they turn merely on an adequate grasp of concepts and issues. The evaluative negativity of certain transactions and circumstances is immediate, perspicuous, self-evident: it is simply a matter of the recognition, available to all morally competent agents as such, that some sorts of situations are painful, unpleasant, incongruous, and unacceptable and thereby constitute negativities. It forms part of the presuppositions of entry into the range of discourse at issue—the individual who does not recognize the infliction of needless avoidable pain as a negativity is someone with whom we cannot hold a meaningful discussion of moral issues.

Certain evaluations are thus simply a matter of an experientially grounded grasp of fundamentals. The propositions that formulate such states of affairs are trivial, truistic, and able to dispense with any need for grounding in something further that supports *ab extra*. For example, the negativity of pain and with it the moral inappropriateness of its deliberate and needless propagation are simply instances of such an evaluative truism.

What marks such an evaluative truism as enthymematically available is not its profound truth but its very triviality. If someone were to dissent from it, we would have no alternative but to take the view that this betrays the absence of any real grasp of the central concepts operative in discussion and deliberation within the domain at issue. We would have to take essentially the same reaction here that we would take toward someone who failed to acknowledge that knives have blades. If someone were to deny that knives have blades we could not take the line that he was overlooking some significant fact about the world, but simply would have to acknowledge that he did not have a firm grasp on what it is to be a knife. Similarly, if someone denied assent to "It is morally wrong to inflict needless pain on people," we would not take the line that he did not have a proper grasp of deep truths about morality, but merely that he simply did not know what morality is all about. The same story holds not only for "causing needless pain," but also in an endless variety of other cases such as taking something that belongs to another simply because we want to have it, on the negative side, and helping someone in a way that involves no loss for other people, on the positive side.

This condition of affairs takes the steam out of a negative resolution of the fact-derivability question in a debate about the subjectivity of values. Even though the inferential transition from facts to values must always make use of some evaluative theses, nevertheless such inferential mediators can be wholly unproblematic truisms that, as such, stand secure from the vagaries of potentially idiosyncratic value appraisals.

Subjectivists accordingly obtain no aid and comfort from recognizing findings that values cannot be derived from facts alone—that explicitly or implicitly evaluative claims are always required to render such argumentation cogent. This circumstance is stripped of any subjectivistic implications by the consideration that the requisite value inputs can be altogether trivial and truistic. On this basis, the prospects of value objectivism are unaffected by a recognition that values cannot be derived from facts.

The reality of it is that descriptive facts and normative facts are more closely interrelated than is generally recognized. They share a common epistemology. Rational cognition and rational evaluation run wholly parallel in point of validation because cognition too is an ultimately evaluative enterprise. Values and descriptive facts are both governed by norms. Our knowledge of both sorts of facts, the descriptively informative and the normative–evaluative, hinges on the criteriological bearing of the question, What merits approbation? To be sure, this overarching question bears a very different construction on each side of the issue, with approbation as acceptance on the side of descriptive information, and approbation as preference on the side of evaluative judgment. But acceptance too is a preference of sorts: an epistemic preference.

Rational appropriateness in the criteriology of cognition is determined as: Those descriptively informative theses or descriptive judgments qualify as rationally acceptable or cognitively valid that optimally systematize our cognitive data, with systematization proceeding under the aegis of descriptively factual generalizations.

In an entirely parallel way, we have the following situation on the side of the criteriology of evaluation: Those normatively evaluative theses or evaluative judgments qualify as rationally acceptable or normatively valid that optimally systematize our evaluative data, with systematization proceeding under the aegis of normative rules.

Both the descriptive and the normative sides begin with the data of experience. In the alethic, descriptively truth-oriented case, these are the data of sensation and their systemic extensions in factual theories. In the evaluative, normatively value-oriented case, these are the data of evaluation—of pro-or-con appraisal and their systemic extensions in normative rules. In both cases we proceed criteriologically in terms of the optimal systematization of experience, by just the same device of seeking the best available extrapolation of the data, the interpretation that best coheres with the rest of our experience.

The parallelism between the two cases is depicted in the display that follows, which portrays a value cognitivism that sees the processes of rational inquiry and of rational evaluation as proceeding in a strictly parallel way. On both sides, system building provides the key for discriminating between what is tenable and what is not. One selfsame fundamental idea of controlling validity through the optimal systematization of the relevant data runs uniformly across both the cognitive and normative domains. In either case, this is a matter of systematization of experience:

- *Cognition*: rational systematization of informative experience through principles of explanation
- *Evaluation*: rational systematization of affective experience through principles of justification

Essentially, the same standard applies throughout: a judgment is valid if it belongs to the optimal, most cogent systematization of the whole range of our relevant, alethically fact-oriented experience on the one side and that of our relevant, axiologically value-oriented experience on the other.

The coherence approach to value criteriology in terms of judgmental systematization accordingly runs wholly parallel to the coherence approach to acceptance criteriology.[2] The parallelism of the systemic process operative in both the cognitive and evaluative sectors engenders a symmetry of validation on the sides of cognitive and evaluative reason that once again exhibits the fundamental unity of reason.

No wonder, then, that altogether analogous issues arise on both the cognitive and the evaluative sides. In the alethic case, we face the problem of bridging a seemingly insuperable gap between appearance and reality, between phenomenally subjective claims at the level of appearances and impressions, and ontologically objective claims at the level of being and actuality. The coherence criteriology of factual truth is of good avail here. It authorizes the inference from claims on the order of "There looks to be a cat on the mat" to claims on the order of "There actually is a cat on the mat" through the optimal systematization of our relevant experience. In making this inference, we exploit the circumstance that this particular ruling regarding the nature of the real best systematizes our cognitive commitments overall. An entirely parallel situation prevails on the evaluative, axiological side, where we face the problem of bridging a seemingly insuperable gap between subjective claims at the level of evaluative feelings and objective claims at the level of actual evaluation—between what seems wicked and what is wicked. Of course what the coherence criteriology of norms enables us to do in this case is to leap across just exactly this gap. It puts us in a position to move from claims on the order of "Stealing seems wicked to me" to claims on the order of "Stealing is wrong" through the mediation of the principle of best systematization.[3]

On both sides of experience, both with the sensory observation and evaluative assessment, we thus leap across the gap separating subjective seeming from objective being by one and the same methodological device, namely, a rational systematization of the data. In each case we enter into a realm of objective claims through triangulation from the data of experience. Of course, the greater extent of the interpersonal uniformity of sensory as compared with evaluative experience makes the case of sensation simpler than that of evaluation. But the difference is one of degree rather than of kind.

This fundamental parallelism means that value issues should also be seen in a "realistic" light. Matters of value too can and should be regarded as objectively factual—the difference is just that we are dealing with evaluative rather than simply informative facts. The possibility of rational agreement, disagreement, criticism, correction, and the like arises on the evaluative side also. We must avoid the confusion of values with tastes. "There's no disputing about tastes" may be true, but "There's no disputing about values" certainly is not. Values too can be altogether objective, in that value claims admit of rational support through impersonally cogent considerations.

To reemphasize: the rational validation of descriptively factual claims in empirical inquiry and of evaluative claims in normative assessment proceed in closely analogous ways. Both consist in the rational systematization of experience, to art, informative and evaluative experience, respectively. The parallelism of alethic and axiological criteriology indicates that what is sauce for the informative–inductive goose is also sauce for the evaluative–normative gander. This circumstance is highly important from the angle of philosophical concerns. For one thing, it illustrates from yet another direction of approach the holistic unity and integrity of reason. For another, it indicates that the very existence of an evaluative sector of reason hinges on the prospects of an objective rational inquiry into the nature and bearing of evaluative considerations. And this is all to the good. Given the systemic unity of reason, the whole of rationality would be at risk if rational deliberation about matters of value were in principle impossible.

## NOTES

This chapter is a revised version of an essay of the same title published in *The Journal of Value Inquiry* 35 (2001): pp. 5–12. Copyright © 2001 Kluwer Academic Publishers. Reprinted by kind permission of Kluwer Academic Publishers.

1. Cf. Judith Jarvis Thomson, introduction to *The Realm of Rights* (Cambridge, Mass.: Harvard University Press, 1990).
2. On coherence criteriology see the author's *The Coherence Theory of Truth* (Oxford: Oxford University Press, 1973), as well as ch. 2, "Truth as Ideal Coherence" in the author's *Forbidden Knowledge* (Dordrecht: Kluwer, 1987), pp. 17–27.
3. For the detail needed to flesh out this telegraphic sketch, see the author's *The Validity of Values* (Princeton, N.J.: Princeton University Press, 1993).

## Chapter Four

# Deliberative Conservatism

Conservatism is usually conceived of as a political ideology favoring the preservation of established social institutions and the maintenance of the political status quo. And as far as it goes, this is all very well. But it does not go very deep. What is actually at issue is something far more deep-rooted and pervasive—something that cuts through to the very foundations of our decision making in every aspect of life.

The crux of the issue roots in the nature of the human situation. The circumstances of our existence are such that many of our decisions—and many of the most important ones—have to be made under conditions of unavoidable uncertainty.

We live in circumstances of extensive ignorance—of a massive insufficiency of information regarding ourselves and our own destinies, regarding our fellows and their doings and dealings, and regarding the world we live in and its complex eventuations. As a result, our actions are in large measure leaps in the dark whose consequences are both unforeseen and unforeseeable. We live in a domain extremely subject to the forces of chance and chaos—of pervasive unpredictability. We all face Hamlet's predicament, the inability to fathom what the consequences of our actions—individual or collective—are actually going to be. There is not only a "fog of war" that bedevils the battlefield of combat but also a "fog of life" that bedevils the battlefield of life in regard to the complex choices that we face upon it.

And so when we deliberate about what to do—even with the best of intentions—we cannot but realize that matters will "aft gang agley." We have to act in this world amidst an inescapable recognition that our decisions can misfire, that even our best-laid and best-intentioned actions can go wrong.

And in particular in seeking to avert or ameliorate some negativity we must always reckon with the prospect that matters can go wrong by way of

- Engendering more of the negativity at issue
- Introducing new negativities (even when the one at issue is reduced)

The measures we select—well planned and well intentioned though they may be—have to be adopted amidst a clear recognition that for unforeseen and unforeseeable reasons matters may possibly just not work out and that in seeking to make things better we have managed to make them worse.

Let $A^+$ be the most promising improvement to the status quo that presents itself to our view in the prevailing circumstances. Then the ruling principle of conservatism is:

Implement $A^+$ only if there is concrete evidence that this will prove successful, and thus do not act in the absence of such evidence.

By contrast, the ruling principle of liberalism is:

Implement $A^+$ if there is no concrete evidence that this will prove unsuccessful.

Conservatism is an injunction to inaction:

No concrete evidence of success $\rightarrow$ Don't do!

Liberalism is an injunction to action:

No concrete evidence of nonsuccess $\rightarrow$ Do!

The one principle mandates inaction in the absence of evidenced adequacy; the other mandates action in the absence of evidential counterindications. Both alike are thus instructions about how to proceed in situations of evidential insufficiency.

But, of course, the procedures at issue are very different, and are based on very different principles of presumption and burden of proof to wit:

- Presume inadequacy unless specific proindications come to view
- Presume adequacy until specific counterindications come to view

The former pessimistic approach is the hallmark of a "conservative" perspective; the latter, optimistic approach is the hallmark of a "liberal" perspective.

Both conservatism and its liberal contrary agree that when there is definite, concrete evidence in favor of an improvement on the status quo, then that settles matters. What they disagree about is how to proceed in the all too common absence of such definite and concrete evidence.

Seen in the light of burden-of-proof considerations, conservatism takes this burden to incline *against* proposed improvements in the status quo. To authorize action it insists on concrete evidence that this will actually succeed in effecting improvements in the status quo. By contrast, liberalism sees the burden of proof as inclining *in favor* of proposed improvements in the status quo. To validate inaction it insists on concrete evidence that this will not succeed in effecting improvements in the status quo.

Conservatism is mindful of the gap between the cup of good situations and the cup of satisfying results. The thought of the many things that can go wrong in human affairs is never far away. And so, the conservative's presumption favors the status quo. He is prepared to make a supposedly positive change only if there is concrete and specific evidence in its favor.

To be sure, the liberalism/conservatism distinction is not *defined* in terms of this variant approach toward reform—here it is a matter of variant views of human claims and even of human prospects in circumstances of social interaction. Nevertheless, these two approaches exhibit different tendencies in matters of reform. If, with conservatives, one takes a pessimistic view of man's perfectibility and consequently acknowledges the need for greater social sanctions and controls, one will be naturally more skeptical of measures that exchange the security of an established status quo for the potentially risky promises of social innovation.

The rational conservative favors the status quo not (necessarily) because he *likes* it but because, being by its very nature a *known quantity*, its features are discerned with confidence. Its negativities are determinate, its deficiencies familiar; its downside, such as it is, lies open for all to see. The uncertainty that may—and generally does—afflict its rivals is absence in it and we know exactly what we have to deal with. Hamlet's predicament is that when a contemplated action carries us into the unknown

> . . . . the native hue of resolution
> Is sicklied o'er with the pale cast of thought,
> And enterprises of great pith and moment
> With this regard their currents turn away,
> And lose the name of action.

> (*Hamlet* III, i56.)

In dealing with the known quantity of the status quo, this sort of fret need not concern us.

By contrast, the liberal makes a presumption in favor of change. He is always prepared to make a supposedly positive change unless there is concrete and specific evidence in its disfavor. When a promising-looking charge is under consideration, the conservative is willing to undertake it only if there is a substantial reason for doing to. The liberal, by contrast, is willing to undertake it whenever there is no substantial reason against doing so. The pivotal difference is one of risk awareness.[1]

Liberalism accordingly finds it easier to put its seal of approval to proposals for change. Its well-intentioned openness to change is in its favor. But its comparative myopia in looking to the potential dangers is what stands in the way of unqualified approbation.

And so, in its root basics, the issue of conservatism versus liberalism is a matter not of a specifically political orientation but rather of an approach toward risk—one not of politico-social polity but of risk-management policy. The liberal is willing to follow the siren call of promising possibility. The conservative is from Missouri. His motto is "Show me!"

One key lesson of the deliberations is clear. The contrast between conservatism and its alternatives is something very pervasive that runs across the board of human decision making in general. Conservatism in its traditional political form is only one particular special instance of a very general idea. These approaches can, of course, become operative in the realm of public decision making and policy formation in political matters of legislation or public policy. But they can also operate across the board in very different areas—in commerce, in personal affairs, in medicine. Conservatism is not so much a political ideology as an attitude toward life—or something toward that particularly prominent sector of it that has to do with the choice among alternatives. Thus, in the end, William Gilbert was right:

> Nature always does contrive
> That every boy and every girl
> That's born into the world alive,
> Is either a little Liberal
> Or else a little Conservative!

But which attitude is actually warranted? What is the sensible basis of procedure? The answer is that it all depends. There is no simple yes or no here.

It depends entirely on conditions and circumstances, specifically with respect to the following issues:

1. As we have seen, both approaches—conservatism and liberalism alike—are policies addressing the issue of how to proceed in the absence of evidence. So—how hard would it be to secure more evidence so as to dispel the evidential fog regarding changes in the status quo?

2. How great is the uncertainty regarding the alternatives to the status quo? With the status quo we know what we are dealing with. What sorts of possibilities arise as we move off in a variant direction and what sorts of hazards do they pose? It is clearly advisable to proceed with caution in the presence of substantial uncertainties on such issues.

3. Just how unsatisfactory is the status quo? Is it so bad that virtually anything else is bound to be an improvement? If the status quo is not all that bad, we can afford to be cautious about changes that involve a leap into the unknown. The precept "If it ain't broke, don't fix it" has the cousin "If it ain't very broke, be cautious about fiddling with it."

4. What risks are going to be run in making that proposed change? How severe is the potential down side? Is there a fair prospect of making matters substantially worse—of leaping from the frying pan into the fire? In the presence of big risks one had best proceed carefully.

5. How volatile is the overall situation in which the status quo and its alternatives are caught up together? In substantially unstable and volatile conditions the status quo becomes unreliable in any case and no alternative can be pursued with firm confidence in its realization. (The whole decision situation is pretty much a crapshoot.) When matters are thus largely beyond rational control, we might as well run potentially hopeful risks and take our chances.

6. What are the relevantly operative probabilities? Even in situations of evidential insufficiency there may be determinable likelihoods (in terms or analogies, for example) to guide our choices.

All of these variant issues regarding the makeup of situations and circumstances can influence the comparative appropriateness of a conservative vs. liberal strategy of decision. And so another key lesson of these deliberations is that if we have a good grasp of the overall situation, we can make a comparatively more sensible decision as to what sort of policy—one of conservation or of liberation—is in order with respect to the issues at hand.

Above all, however, it will depend on the size of the stake and on the nature of the risk at issue. Desperate circumstances call for desperate measures. Any port in a storm! To avert catastrophe we should clutch at any straws: however small the chances of success. Whatever is our only chance for catastrophe prevention—however modest be its credentials—deserves the presumption of efficacy.

Strange though it may seem, liberalism is a policy best suited to desperate times. But under ordinary conditions—amidst the usual conditions of everyday life when circumstances are ordinary rather than extreme and the situations are modest rather than massive—the pathway of a more cautious conservation would seem to have much in its favor.

And so here the paramount lesson of these deliberations emerges. On the issue of conservatism versus liberalism, there simply is no one-size-fits-all solution. Which policy is the sensitive one to adopt will depend on the nature of the case—on the character conditions and circumstances that define the situation at hand. The question of appropriateness in this regard is simply not one that admits of a uniform, across-the-board answer.

## NOTE

1. Cf. Kenneth J. Arrow, *Essays on the Theory of Risk-Bearing* (Clarage: Morkham, 1971), and J. W. Pralt, "Risk Aversion in the Small and the Large," *Econometrics* 32 (1964): pp. 122–36.

*Chapter Five*

# Predictive Incapacity and Rational Decision

## 1. RATIONALITY AND PREDICTABILITY

The acts of rational agents are usually predictable because it is often and perhaps even usually possible to figure out on the basis of general principles what the rational thing to do is in the prevailing situation. This circumstance makes rationality into a crucial predictive resource in matters of human action. Indeed, it is on just this basis that we try to understand people, since we ordinarily credit them with being rational until such time as they prove themselves otherwise. In consequence, the actions of free agents must be substantially predictable—if they are rational, at any rate.

To be sure, rationality can—in some special cases—also provide an advantage-engendering antidote to predictability. Suppose that there were a forecasting device designed to predict your actions. If it were possible for you to discern the device's modus operandi, then you could always defeat its predictions by first figuring out what it will predict you to do, and then doing something else. Clearly, an effective predictive mechanism forecasting the actions of a free agent—someone who is fully master of her own actions—would have to be opaque to that agent, with its operations substantially inscrutable to her, since otherwise she could systematically frustrate the predictor.[1] But even agents who cannot fathom a predictor's proceedings and thereby frustrate its operations can nevertheless still defeat it by the simple strategy of being *unpredictable*, by choosing their actions haphazardly—with the aid of a random device if need be. To be sure, a sufficiently competent predictor could predict this very fact—"She'll proceed randomly on this one." But in the circumstances *this* particular sort of predictive success at the procedural level would not—could not—enable a prediction to forecast the agent's specific choice or action.

Moreover, acting unpredictably is not cost free. Rational agents will, by hypothesis, proceed by figuring out what is the sensible (the best or most appropriate) thing to do in the circumstances. And their predictability can thus be defeated only at the price of sometimes doing something suboptimal, something that departs from what would otherwise be the course of reason.

In the ordinary course of things, predictability is integral to rationality. To recognize someone as a fellow rational being is to see their behavior as predictable by us and by them alike—to commit oneself to expecting that person to do much the same as we ourselves (or indeed *any* rational being) would do in the same circumstances. Predictability is a *coordination* principle, a means for aligning the choice-involving (and thus future-contemplating) proceedings of different agents so as to render their ongoing activities mutually understandable. The need for harmonious coexistence—for coordinating the actions of independent agents—explains why the predictability of (the bulk of) its members is an indispensable asset in any human community. For this very reason evolutionary considerations dictate the presence of this feature—if the community did not have it, and use it by and large, then the community would likely not be there owing to its inability to function effectively.

Nevertheless, while we humans qualify (so we cannot but suppose) as rational agents who as such are predictively tractable, we are also feckless creatures, often exercising our free agency in an erratic, willful, inconsequent, haphazard manner. Accordingly, even when we know people well, and understand their tastes, dispositions, and inclinations, we sometimes, at least, cannot foretell with confidence what they—or actually even we ourselves—will do in particular circumstances. And so, our human capacity for reason-geared agency must be seen as double-edged, able both to promote and to impede predictability.

## 2. PREDICTIVE OVERDETERMINATION: THE CASE OF THE PREDICTIVE POISONER

Reliable prediction of what rational agents do will clearly be impracticable when we have insufficient information regarding the circumstances at issue. If I do not know about Jane's tastes, I cannot predict what dish she will select from the menu. If I know nothing about a stranger's background when wandering about in the United Nations Headquarters, I cannot predict what language he will speak when he opens his mouth. Incompleteness of information will *underdetermine* outcomes and thereby preclude rational prediction about the doings of even ideally rational agents. And seeing that one's information about even fully rational agents is invariably incomplete, circumstances will preclude their predictability.

The unpredictability of rational agency has another domain, however. Besides the situation of *informational underdetermination,* there is also the problem of *analysis overdetermination*. This turns on the prospect of equally plausible but nevertheless divergent rational assessments regarding the actions of a rational agent in given circumstances. The problem here is not one of insufficient data to support a plausible analysis to substantiate a prediction, but rather one of there being a surfeit of such analyses all pointing in very different directions. This sort of situation is less well recognized and theoretically more interesting. Let us consider some examples.

Consider the problem posed by a friend of yours (Dr. Psychic Psycho), an otherwise intelligent, serious, reliable, and generally sagacious and self-assured individual who fancies himself a clairvoyant psychic and indeed has a good track record for oddball predictions. After you have just eaten apples together, he proceeds to astonish you with the following announcement:

"I have interesting news for you. You must seriously consider taking this pill. As you know (since we have recently determined it together) it contains substance *X,* which (as you also know—but consult this pharmacopoea if in doubt) is fatally poisonous by itself, but nevertheless is an unfailing antidote to poison *Z*—though it does have some minorly unpleasant side effects. Now the apple I gave to you, which you have just finished eating, was poisoned by me with *Z* in line with my prediction as to your taking or not taking the antidote pill. Benign old me of course only poisoned the apple if I foresaw that you were indeed going to take the antidote. And not to worry—I'm a very good predictor."

At this point your strange friend rushes off and vanishes from the scene. Any prospect of beating the truth out of him disappears with his departure. And an awful feeling comes over you—you cannot but believe him. In fact, you strongly suspect that he went through the whole rigamarole to get you to take that problem pill. What do you do?[2] Your very life seems to depend on predicting the result of taking that pill.

Of course you proceed to do a quick bit of decision theory. For starters, you map out the spectrum of available possibilities:

| You | He | According to Him/You | Your System Contains | Result |
|---|---|---|---|---|
| take | predicts correctly | take | Z, X | survive |
| take | predicts incorrectly | not take | X | die |
| not take | predicts correctly | not take | | survive |
| not take | predicts incorrectly | take | Z | die |

Not a pretty picture. After all, you stand a chance of dying whether or not you take that accursed pill. What to do?

Two lines of analysis are available here:

## Analysis 1

Let $p$ = probability that he correctly predicts your action. In terms of an expectation-of-life measure, we now have:

$$EV \text{ (take)} = p \, (+\, 1^-) + (1-p) \, (-\, 1)$$

$$EV \text{ (not take)} = p \, (+\, 1) + (1-p) \, (-\, 1)$$

Here we clearly have it that $EV$ (take) $< EV$ (not take), irrespective of the value of $p$. (Note that the small superscripted minus sign ($^-$) means "a smidgeon less" and comes into play owing to the minor negative side effect of taking the pill.)

On this basis, the expected-value comparison envisioned in orthodox decision theory appears to rule against taking that pill, quite independently of any estimate of how good a predictor Dr. Psycho is or isn't.

## Analysis 2

Let $p$ = probability that he actually poisoned the apple. We now have:

$$EV \text{ (take)} = p \, (+\, 1^-) + (1-p) \, (-\, 1) = 2p - (-1)$$

$$EV \text{ (not take)} = p \, (-\, 1) + (1-p) \, (+\, 1) = -2p + 1$$

Note that:

$EV$ (take) $> EV$ (not take) whenever:

$$(2p)^- - 1 > -2p + 1$$

$$(4p)^- > 2$$

$$p > (\tfrac{1}{2})^+$$

Now let it be that, in addition to the given information, you strongly suspect (*ex hypothesi*) that he went through this bizarre exercise to induce you to take the pill (which presumably to his sight, you will do iff he poisons the apple). Then clearly the preceding condition on $p$ is satisfied, and you are decision-theoretically well advised to take the pill.

Which of these two discordant analyses is right? That is difficult to say—indeed effectively impossible. On the available indications both available alternatives seem perfectly cogent. Comparably plausible arguments pro and con can be given either way. You pay your money and take your choice—or toss your coin.

The predictive problem at issue—What is the consequence of taking the pill? Which way lies the course of safety?—is one where decision-theoretic rationality is *overdeterminative*, as it were, and thereby analytically indecisive. We confront a situation where distinct, equally cogent and equally plausible-looking analyses lead to different resolutions. Discordant predictions are rationally validatable and the abstract case that can be made for the one is every bit as good as that which can be made for the other. In consequences, the prospect of rational prediction eludes us here on grounds of analysis overdetermination.

As is clear from the existence of interaction games such as rock, paper, scissors in contrast to tic-tac-toe, there sometimes is no effective strategy of play apart from brute random choice. No analysis of the range of options indicates one option to be superior to the rest: every alternative that confronts one has as much to be said for (or against) it as any other. Here analysis *underdetermines* the choice of an advisable resolution: there are no good arguments for selecting one possibility over against some other alternative. The present situation is, as it were, a cousin to that one. There are good arguments for one resolution, but unfortunately they are matched by equally good arguments for another. In both cases alike it accordingly becomes impossible to predict with warranted confidence how even an ideally rational agent would proceed.

## 3. ANOTHER CASE OF ANALYSIS UNDERDETERMINATION: THE PRISONER'S DILEMMA

This general sort of predicament is not all that unusual. Yet another, more familiar illustration of it is the situation of the well-known "Prisoner's Dilemma," which stands as follows: You and your accomplice *A* have committed some crime. The two of you are eventually arrested and charged. The public prosecutor offers you a plea bargain: Confess and turn state's evidence against your accomplice and she will ensure that the courts will treat you leniently—provided that your confession turns out to be useful for her case. Note further: (1) The utility of your confession depends on whether your accomplice keeps silent. (If he does, your confession is valuable, but if he too confesses, the value of your confession is reduced.) (2) If neither of you confesses, then the prosecutor's case is in fact so weak that both of you will almost certainly get off scott-free.

On this basis, you will confront the following spectrum of possibilities.

| Your Choice | Your Accomplice's Choice | Your Preference | Your Accomplice's Preference |
|---|---|---|---|
| confess | confess | 3 | 3 |
| confess | not confess | 1 | 4 |
| not confess | confess | 4 | 1 |
| not confess | not confess | 2 | 2 |

This overall setup yields the following interaction matrix, where the entry $x / y$ indicates a result of $x$ for you and one of $y$ for your accomplice:

|  | Accomplice's Choice | |
|---|---|---|
| Your Choice | confess | not confess |
| confess | 3 / 3 | 1 / 4 |
| not confess | 4 / 1 | 2 / 2 |

Note that from your perspective any choice you make has both promises and risks, so that your preferred choice pivots critically on your prediction of what your accomplice will do. But what is the answer here? What will he do?

Again, two variant lines of analysis lie at one's disposal:

## Analysis 1

Note that dominance considerations come into operation. Observe that if your accomplice (or indeed either party to the interaction) confesses, then this party is comparatively the better off irrespective of what the other party does. Clearly, confession seems indicated. Accordingly, one would predict that your accomplice, being rational, will choose confession. (And then you had better do the same.) Thus, on this basis, both of you are impelled to confess. And this mutual confession leads the two of you to forgo the prospect of getting off scott-free. Here your prediction ("Being a rational agent, he is bound to confess") impels you to a clearly suboptimal result.

## Analysis 2

Under the circumstances, you are seeking for a rational resolution of the prediction problem posed by the situation. And so is your accomplice. But note that you are both in exactly the same predicament: the situation is completely symmetric. To whatever extent you are rationally impelled to a certain reso-lution, so is he. Hence, the only realistically available outcomes are those that lie on the diagonal and have both of you doing the same thing. And on this basis, not confessing is clearly optimal by way of utility maximization. So now you predict that in searching for a rational resolution your accomplice is also going to realize this and will not confess.[3]

Here again, two perfectly cogent-seeming analyses point in diametrically op-posite directions. Once more we confront a situation of rational prediction that is intractable on grounds of an overabundance of divergent lines of analysis.[4]

## 4. LESSONS

The examples considered here convey a clear lesson. Predictive situations can arise in which the resources of rational reflection fail us, and do so for reasons other than a gross insufficiency in the information needed to support a sensible resolution. One can also fall into perplexity in informationally de-terminate situations where several equally cogent modes of analysis lead to discordant and conflicting resolutions. With analysis overdetermination, the predicament is genuinely *aporetic* in that it makes for a *conflict of argu-ments,* with equally plausible lines of reflection pointing in diametrically op-posed directions.

It is an essential feature of the situations at issue with predictive overde-termination that they involve the *interaction of rational agents* in situations of choice. In interactions with *nature*, the dialectical disability that arises in the examples could not arise. A balance of forces creates equilibrium and in-action; a balance of reasons leaves room for the arbitrariness of free agency. (This presumably was the object of the notorious medieval example of Buri-dan's ass.[5]) It is a significant feature of human rationality that while its very reason for being is to render the actions of free agents more predictable it nonetheless brings in its wake an unpredictability of potential under- and overdetermination that provides not only a place but even a need for free (ar-bitrary, unpredictable) choice.

The crux, however, is that, in choice situations of the Buridan's ass type that present alternatives with equal merit on all sides—as with the game of rock, paper, scissors—the choices of a rational agent are ipso facto unpre-dictable. Here arbitrary random selection is the best available option. And this circumstance marks the limit of rational predictability in such cases: where rational agents cannot determine optional solutions, rational predictors cannot for this very reason predict their responses.

There is no gainsaying the predictively most useful principle that rational agents will—given the chance—do just exactly what is rationally optimal for them in their circumstances. But for reasons of lack of information or of analytical undetermination the quest for a *unique* optimal resolution may be unavailing: we may, in the end, be left with equally eligible alternatives. And at this point—where uniqueness fails even after rationality has had its say—the predictive efficacy of that otherwise useful guiding principle is lost. In situations where people face a rational choice between equivalent alternatives the resources of rationality will thereby become predictively unavailing. But fortunately for us (though unfortunately for predictors) mere arbitrary *choice* can provide resolutions that lie beyond the dictates of reason. For better or worse, human decision can break the ties that result when for one reason or another the voice of reason is simply indecisive.

## NOTES

This chapter was originally published in *The European Review* 3 (1995): pp. 327–32. Reprinted by kind permission of the publisher.

1. For an informative discussion of such *counterpredictive* comportment see Michael Scriven, "An Essential Unpredictability in Human Behavior," in *Scientific Psychology*, ed. B. B. Wolman (New York: Basic Books, 1965), pp. 411–25.

2. This problem is a distant cousin of Newcomb's problem, for which see Robert Nozick, "Newcomb's Problem and Two Principles of Choice" in *Essays in Honor of Carl G. Hempel*, ed. N. Rescher (Dordrecht: D. Reidel, 1969). In its original version, this problem involves a head-on collision between the two prime principles of rational decision: dominance and expected-utility maximization. The Dr. Psycho problem, however, involves a clash of two different but equally plausible ways of implementing the process of expected-value maximization.

3. A wide spectrum of approaches to resolving the Prisoner's Dilemma problem is discussed in Richmond Campbell and Lanning Sowden, eds., *Paradoxes of Rationality and Cooperation* (Vancouver: University of British Columbia Press, 1985). The literature represented includes analysts who argue each side of the issue with comparable plausibility. The editors consider (pp. 10–11) the prospect that rationality as such may simply fail to determine a unique solution, but unaccountably regard this as a matter of "blaming rationality." It does not occur to them that this makes about as much sense as "blaming rationality" for failing to provide a unique solution to $x^2 - 1 = 0$. We cannot ask rationality to provide uniqueness in circumstances where it is absent: *ultra posse nemo obligatur*.

4. Various problems that are comparably analysis indeterminate also exist in the literature—for example, Newcomb's problem for which see Nozick, "Newcomb's Problems and Two Principles of Choice," pp. 178–97. Other comparable "prediction paradoxes" are discussed in Jean-Paul Delabaye, "Machines, prédictions, et fin du monde," *Pour la science*, no. 191 (September 1993): pp. 96–103. See also W. Poundstone, *Labyrinths of Reason* (New York: Andiron-Doubleday, 1990), pp. 248–53.

5. See the chapter on "Choice without Preference" in the author's *Essays in Philosophical Analyses* (Pittsburgh: University of Pittsburgh Press, 1969).

*Chapter Six*

# Dismissing Extremely Remote Possibilities

## 1. INTRODUCTION

Investigators of the theory of knowledge have long recognized and emphasized that there are significant differences between theoretical and practical reason, between reason's modus operandi in solving purely theoretical problems (where nothing save the possibility of mistaken beliefs is at risk) and its modus operandi in resolving practical issues (where actual harm of some sort might be incurred). There is, however, no more striking illustration of this situation than the little heeded issue of the treatment of remote possibilities—those whose probability is *extremely* small. Here the question before us is this: In regard to matters of practice, should a diminutive probability (one of an effectively infinitesimal magnitude ∈) be seen as being indistinguishable from zero and treated as something that has no magnitude at all. In our deployment of probabilities in using expected value comparisons as guides for decision making could and should we adopt the equation: $\epsilon = 0$?[1]

## 2. EFFECTIVELY ZERO PROBABILITIES

A probability has to be a quantity between zero and one. Now, numbers between zero and one can be very small indeed: As $N$ gets bigger, $1/N$ will grow very, very small. What, then, is one to do about extremely small probabilities in the rational management of risks?[2]

On this issue there is a systemic disagreement between probabilists working on theory-oriented issues in mathematics or natural science and decision theorists who work on practical decision-oriented issues relating to human affairs.

The former takes the line that small numbers are small numbers and must be taken into account as such—that is, as the small quantities they actually are. The latter tend to take the view that small probabilities represent extremely remote prospect and can be written off. (*De minimis non curat lex*, as the old precept has it: in human affairs there is no need to bother with trifles.) When something is about as probable as a thousand fair dice when tossed a thousand times coming up all sixes, then, so it is held, we can pretty well forget about it as worthy of concern. As a matter of practical policy, we operate with probabilities on the principle that when $x \leq \epsilon$, then $x = 0$. We take the line that in our human dealings in real-life situations a sufficiently remote possibility can—for all sensible purposes—be viewed as being of probability zero.

Accordingly, such remote possibilities can simply be dismissed, and the outcomes with which they are associated can accordingly be set aside. And in "the real world" people do in fact seem to be prepared to treat certain probabilities as effectively zero, taking certain sufficiently improbable eventualities as no longer representing *real* possibilities.[3]

Here an extremely improbable event is seen as something we can simply write off as being outside the range of appropriate concern, something we can dismiss for all practical purposes. As one writer on insurance puts it:

[P]eople . . . refuse to worry about losses whose probability is below some threshold. Probabilities below the threshold are treated as though they were zero.[4]

No doubt, remote-possibility events having such a minute possibility *can* happen in some sense of the term, but this "can" functions somewhat figuratively—it is no longer seen as something that presents a realistic prospect.

In epistemic contexts, as David Lewis has pointed out, the assignment of probability zero or one indicates "absolute certainty [that] is tantamount to a firm resolution never to change your mind, no matter what."[5] However, in the practicalistic use of decision theory in contexts of choosing courses of action, setting a probability at zero means no more than ruling the corresponding possibility out provisionally, pro tem, as an object of appropriate concern in the situation at hand. The significance of such a probability annihilation is something rather different in these two contexts of deliberation.

To be sure, it needs to be stressed that in practical contexts, such a treatment of the probabilities at issue is essentially a matter of fiat—of deciding that as a matter of policy a certain level of sufficiently low probability can be taken as a cut off point below which we are no longer dealing with *real* possibilities and with *genuine* risks.

Of course, this recourse to effective zerohood does not represent a strictly objective, factual circumstance. (After all, $\epsilon = 0$ is a literal falsehood.) It reflects a matter of choice or decision, namely, the *practical* step of treating certain theoretically extant possibilities as unreal—as not worth bothering about, as being literally *negligible* and meriting being set at zero. It is not that those minimalities do not exist, but that we need not trouble ourselves about them because of the improbability of matters going wrong. We can, in brief, dismiss them from the range of practical concern. After all, we are, by hypothesis, operating with issues in the practical rather than theoretical domain.

It thus needs to be emphasized that the thesis $\in\ =0$ is not being adopted as a factual contention and thereby as involving us in a useful error (*felix culpa*) of some sort. It is not a matter of a useful, albeit erroneous claim, but of a *practical policy* procedure The situation is akin to that of statements such as "In the absence of specific counterindications, accept what people say as true." Taken as a thesis of fact (with "accept" deleted and "as" replaced by "is") the claim is false. But it could, nevertheless, prove to be useful and productive as a practical policy.

## 3. HOW SMALL IS SMALL ENOUGH?

Of course, the question remains: How small is small enough for being "effectively zero"? With what value of $\in$ does $\in\ =0$ begin: just exactly where does the threshold of effective zerohood lie?

This is clearly not something that can be resolved in a once-and-for-all manner. It may vary from case to case and possibly even from individual to individual, changing with the "cautiousness" of the person involved, representing an aspect of an individual's stance toward the whole risk-taking process. And it may also be taken to vary with the magnitude of the stake at issue. It seems plausible to allow the threshold of effective zerohood to reflect the magnitude of the threat at issue, taking lower values as the magnitude of the stake at issue increases. (Such a policy seems in smooth accord with the fundamental principle of risk management that greater potential losses should be risked only when their chances for realization are less.)

The empirical facts seem to indicate that in deliberating about risks to human life, for example, there is some tendency to take as a baseline a person's chance of death by natural disasters (or "acts of God"), roughly 1/1,000,000 per annum in the United States. This would be seen as something akin to the "noise level" of a physical system, and fatality probabilities significantly smaller than this would thus be seen as negligible. Such an approach seems to underlay the Food and Drug Administration's proposed, rather more conservative standard of "one in 1 million over a lifetime."[6] People's stance in the face of the probability that when embarking on a commercial airplane trip they will end up as an aviation fatality (which stood at roughly one in 300 million in the United States prior to September 11, 2001) also illustrates this perspective. (Most people neither worry nor insure unless "the company pays.")

To be sure, one important point must be noted in this connection. The probability values that we treat as effectively zero must be values of which, in themselves, we are very sure indeed. But real-life probability values are seldom all that precise. And so in general there will be considerable difficulty in sustaining the judgment that a certain probability indeed is effectively zero. A striking instance is afforded by the Atomic Energy Commission-sponsored "Rasmussen report" of the 1970s (named after Norman C. Rasmussen, the study director) on the accident risks of nuclear power plants:

> From the viewpoint of a person living in the general vicinity of a reactor, the likelihood of being killed in any one year in a reactor accident is one chance in 300,000,000 and the likelihood of being injured in any one year in a reactor accident is one chance in 150,000,000.[7]

The theoretical calculations that sustain such a finding invoke so many assumptions regarding facts, circumstances, and operating principles that such probability estimates are extremely shaky. Outside the domain of purely theoretical science we are too readily plunged below the threshold of experimental error, and will thus confront great difficulties in supporting minute probability distinctions in the sphere of technological and social applications. Statistical probabilities can be very problematic in this regard, in particular since statistical data are often deficient or unavailable in the case of very rare events. Personal probabilities—mere guesses, that is to say—are also very vulnerable in this context of assessing very low probabilities. (For example, the flood victims interviewed by the geographer R. W. Kates flatly denied that flood could ever recur in their area, erroneously attributing previous floods to freak combinations of circumstances that were extremely unlikely to recur.[8]) One writer has maintained that in safety-engineering contexts it simply is not possible to construct sufficiently convincing arguments to support very small probabilities (below $10^5$).[9] Moreover, it is sometimes tempting to exaggerate the extent to which a distinct possibility is remote. And indeed a diversified literature has been devoted to describing the ways in which the estimation of very low probabilities can go astray.[10] So there is ample room for due caution in this regard.

## 4. WHY ACCEPT A THRESHOLD OF "EFFECTIVE ZEROHOOD"?

In treating subminimal probabilities as negligible and seeing those infinitesimal quantities as effectively null we set a threshold beneath which those diminutive probabilities can be set at zero. But why adopt such a probability threshold—why treat sufficiently remote hazards as simply unreal? What justifies this bit of seeming unrealism?

The idea of treating very small probabilities as effectively zero goes back a long way—to Buffon in the seventeenth century and Cournot in the eighteenth.[11] This stratagem treats certain eventuations as *moral* impossibilities and their nonrealization as *moral* certainties (in the traditional terminology, for which one might substitute the designation of *practical*.) The original motivation for adopting a threshold of effective zerohood arose out of Daniel Bernoulli's "St. Petersburg paradox" set by the following imaginary game:[12]

A fair coin is to be tossed until a head appears. If it does so on the *n*th toss, the gambler is then to be paid $2^n$ ducats. How much should the gambler be prepared to pay to enter the game?

It is easy to see that the mathematical expectation of this gamble is

$$\sum_{n=1}^{\infty} (2^n) \times (\tfrac{1}{2})^n$$

which is clearly infinite. So by the usual standards the gambler should be willing to pay any finite stake, however large. This is clearly counterintuitive. And so Buffon proposed to resolve this problem by emphasizing that the probability $(\tfrac{1}{2})^n$ soon becomes very small indeed for increasing *n*. Once the stage is reached where these small-probability eventuations are seen as "effectively impossible," the mathematical expectation of return becomes finite, and the paradox is resolved.

There are, to be sure, other and perhaps better ways of overcoming this particular obstacle.[13] But the paradox is not the only reason for dismissing remote possibilities. Yet another reason for dismissing subminimally improbable possibilities is that there are just too many of them to cope with in practical terms. To be asked to reckon with such remote possibilities is to baffle our thought by sending it on a chase after endless alternatives.

And there are yet more pressing reasons for dismissing sufficiently improbable possibilities. This lies in our need and desire to avoid stultifying action. It is simply human nature to dismiss sufficiently remote eventualities in one's personal calculations.

The "Vacationer's Dilemma" of figure 6.1 illustrates this phenomenon. Only by dismissing certain sufficiently remote catastrophic misfortunes as outside the range of *real* possibilities—by treating them as negligible—can one avoid the stultification of action on anything like a standard decision-making approach represented by expected-value calculations. The vacationer takes the plausible

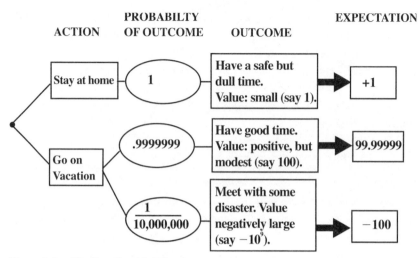

**Figure 6.1.  The Vacationer's Dilemma**

*Note:* The expectation is here the product of the probability of the outcome times its value. Thus for the bottom line we have $10^{-7} \times -10^9 = -100$.

line of viewing the chance of disaster as effectively zero, thereby eliminating that unacceptable possible outcome from playing a role by way of intimidation. People generally (and justifiedly) proceed on the assumption that the probability of sufficiently unlikely disasters can be set at zero; that in certain common-life contexts unpleasant eventuations of extreme improbability can be dismissed as lying outside the realm of "real" or "practical" possibilities. Worrying about extremely remote possibilities—even of quite substantial disasters—simply makes life too difficult.[14] So here fitness considerations seem to favor the dismissal of extremely remote possibilities, seeing that this enables us to keep our practice within the framework of expectation-based decision theory without having to take anomalous and counterintuitive results in stride.

We thus see that the dismissal of extremely remote possibilities will in some cases have its advantages. A reliance on the standard mechanisms of decision theory will in some circumstances no longer be sensible unless we are prepared to dismiss extremely small probabilities as zero.[15] Without some such practical policy, mathematical expectation is no longer a safe and sensible guide to rational decision in such extreme situations.

To be sure, there are also situations in which we incur a disadvantage when we set $\epsilon = 0$. Thus, consider the situation of figure 6.2, which pictures the situation of a person confronted with the choice of paying $X$ to enter a lottery with a one-in-a-million chance of winning a prize of a million dollars or abstaining from this gamble. Since the expected value of entering is

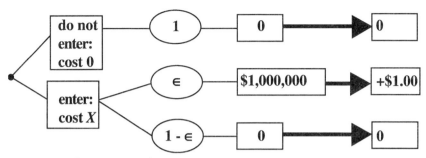

**Figure 6.2.** The Lottery Perplex
*Note:* $\in = 10^{-6}$

$1.00, the subject would, on classical principles, be enjoined to enter the lottery if the cost of doing so were 99¢ (or less). On the other hand, if we adopted the idea of setting $\in = 0$ then the expected value comparison will balance out at 0, so that on classical decision principles our agent would be entirely indifferent between the alternatives.

In the Vacationer's Dilemma our subject would forego a highly probable benefit in the face of risks of an infinitesimally probable disaster. But in the Lottery Perplex our subject is led by this policy to the prospect of paying a sure (albeit modest) price for the sake of an opportunity for a substantial albeit most improbable windfall. The idea of setting $\in = 0$ does not look all that attractive from this latter standpoint.

## 5. THE QUESTION OF VALIDATION

The very issue before us can itself be viewed in a decision-theoretic perspective. In addressing such decision problems we implicitly also confront a second-order decision problem, namely, that of deciding whether to employ the policy $R^+$ of setting $\in = 0$ or to employ the policy $R^-$ of not doing so. Proceeding at this point in the orthodox way we make the expected-value calculation in both ways and then compare. Thus, consider the situation of the Vacationer's Dilemma as per figure 6.3. Viewed on this basis the second alternative clearly looks better than the first on grounds of dominance, so that $R^+$ is in order.

But by contrast consider the structure of the Lottery Perplex as per figure 6.4. Here the first alternative looks to be more attractive than the second seeing that enter or not, we never lose out by following its counsel. And so $R^-$ obtains the advantage and is in order in this case.

The point is that the issue of setting $\in = 0$ is itself a decision issue of procedural choice in such situations.

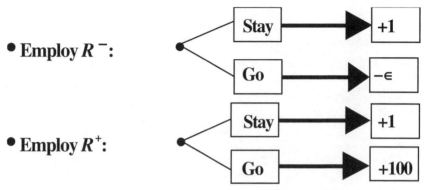

**Figure 6.3.   The Vacationer's Dilemma at the Methodological Level**

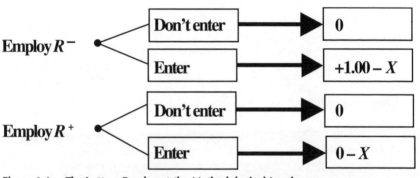

**Figure 6.4.   The Lottery Perplex at the Methodological Level**

## 6. OVERCOMING A PROBLEM

To be sure, a big problem looms on the horizon. The fact of it is that a substantial accumulation of minute chances can become significant.[16] Thus, if we routinely take the step of setting $\in = 0$ for diminutive $\in$, then consider a vast roulette wheel with a zillion compartments, so that the probability that the outcome will lie in any given compartment is less than some diminutive $\in$.

Then on the one hand we have

The probability that the outcome will be in one of those compartments is 1.

While on the other hand since the outcome for each compartment is 0, and 0 5 (anything) = 0, we are committing ourselves to

The probability that the outcome will be one of those compartments 0 5 (the number of compartments), that is to say 0.

By repeating this reasoning once for each compartment, we reach the result that "the probability that the outcome will be in one of these compartments is zero." And this is clearly at variance with our initial finding. Our policy of setting diminutive probabilities to zero has plunged us into a contradiction. How is one to come to terms with this inconsistency?

The step of equating $\in$ with 0 is something we can indulge in only once within the overall decision context at issue.[17] To do this repeatedly would be a matter of having too much of a good thing. Here as elsewhere overindulgence can prove the road to disaster. A proposition claiming an outcome whose probability becomes 1 when we set $\in = 0$ will be said to be *virtually certain*. And as the Lottery Paradox shows, a conjunction of such propositions may *or may not* itself turn out to be virtually certain.

Accordingly, we can now lay claim to the following principle of practical deliberation:

In contexts of practical reasoning—but here only—it is acceptable to include among the premises one—but only one!—virtually certain proposition.

To be sure, sometimes a number of cases can be folded into one. So realistically speaking once will, almost always, be enough. But it will, in general, not be enough to make it possible to engender problems of the sort at issue in the Lottery Perplex.

It may seem odd to contemplate a rule of procedure that can be used only a limited number of times. But an analogy may help to make this restoration more plausible. Consider the rule of practice at issue in the abbreviative convention: in writing omit every fourth letter (counting a space as a letter). Let us apply it to the sentence at the beginning of this paragraph.

IT*MAY*SEEM*ODD*TO*CONTEMPLATE*A*RULE*OF*PROCEDURE

In implementing that suppression rule one arrives at:

IT*AY*EEMODDTO*ONTMPLTE**RUE*O*PRCEDRE

Here it is (perhaps just) possible for a reasonably clever person to figure out what is being said. But it is left as an exercise for the reader to verify that matters are reduced to a hopeless condition when the rule is applied twice over in dealing with the same text.

In just this way, the policy of setting $\epsilon = 0$ is something that must be employed not only with caution and discretion but also with rarity. Indeed: *it is a practical device that one can afford to use only once in the course of addressing a given problem.*

There are various viable practices that can be stretched too far—practical resources whose *repeated* use may, rather than being helpful, work to defeat the purpose at hand. The dismissal of minute possibilities is simply yet another instance of this larger phenomenon.

# 7. CONCLUSION

Clearly we cannot always and everywhere proceed on the somewhat delusional basis that $\epsilon = 0$. But this, of course, does not mean that we should not expect to get away with it on the exceptional occasion. After all, we must not lose sight of the consideration that setting $\epsilon$ at 0 is not a theoretical fact but a practical resource.

In life we have to take risks. And a ruling maxim of sensible procedure here is inherent in the following practical policy:

If proceeding $X$-wise is advantageous or convenient and only very rarely leads to error or difficulty, then it is sensible and appropriate to proceed in this way.

Setting $\epsilon = 0$ follows under exactly this practical policy—indeed is something of a quintessential instance of its operation.

In the final analysis it needs to be acknowledge that there are three sorts of decision situations:

1. *Normal situations* where the standard process of expected value comparison can be applied in the usual way
2. *Catastrophe-threatening situations* where there are risks we would not want to run no matter how small the probability invoked
3. *Extremely remote probability situations* in which we would choose to apply the dismissive ($\epsilon = 0$) tactic dismissed above

And the problem of course is that of deciding how to proceed in situations that fall into both of the last two categories. The dilemma here is that there is unfortunately no way of deciding on principles of abstract reason alone which way to go. There is no objective fact of the matter in classifying a given situation in group two or group three. The resolution has to be made on the basis of what is no more (but also no less) than a judgment call. We pays our money and we takes our choice—and then have no alternative but to live with the consequences. Given the realities regarding our choices in the management of practical affairs this is the best that we can do. And it is neither feasible nor reasonable to set out to do more than the realizable best. Here as elsewhere practical reason has no rational alternative but to proceed with the limits that theoretical reason imposes.

And yet another lesson emerges. Immensely useful tool though it is, rational decision theory has its limits. Its very nature lies in conjuring with probabilities and utilities—in performing articulations with the parameters here at issue. But there can and will arise circumstances and situations—and important ones at that—where these quantities cannot be had. And furthermore, where this impracticality exists it does so not just owing to practical difficulties in making the quantitative determinations in the circumstances at issue, but where there just is no fact of the matter regarding the quantities at issue—where those practicalities and utilities cannot be measured because they just are not defined. In such situations there is no viable alternative to the use of informal rather than formal procedures and to a reliance on judgment calls rather than calculations. In such cases calculation provides no substitute for common sense.

## NOTES

1. Some of the issues of this chapter are also discussed in my 1983 book, *Risk* (Lanham, Md.: University Press of America), see pp. 35–40. I am grateful to Ben Eggleston for constructive comments on a draft of this chapter.

2. Recent probability theorists concerned with inductive issues have dealt with infinitesimal probabilities almost exclusively in the context of the probability of scientific generalizations and laws. (See Richard C. Jeffrey, *The Logic of Decision*, 2d ed. (Chicago & London: University of Chicago Press, 1983), pp. 190–95; and John Earman, *Bayes or Bust* (Cambridge Mass.: MIT Press, 1992) pp. 86–95). This issue of the epistemic acceptability of propositions is of course something rather different from that of the action-guiding concerns of decision theory.

3. In theory this idea of a threshold of effective zerohood can lead to anomalies when the whole spectrum of possibility is covered by a mass of such improbable eventuations. (The so-called Lottery Perplex is an example. See Henry E. Kyburg Jr., *Probability and the Logic of Rational Belief* (Middletown, Conn.: Wesleyan University Press, 1961.) But this theoretical worry is rendered harmless by the fact that most real-life situations do not take this problematic form. (Compare also section 4, "Why Accept a Threshold of 'Effective Zerohood.'")

4. Paul Slovic et al., "Preference for Insuring against Probable Small Losses: Insurance Implications," *The Journal of Risk and Insurance* 44 (1977): pp. 237–58 (see p. 254).

5. David Lewis, "Causal Decision Theory," *Australasian Journal of Philosophy* 59 (1981): p. 14.

6. U.S. Food and Drug Administration, "Chemical Compounds in Food-processing Animals. Criteria and Procedures for Evaluating Assays of Carcinogenic Residues" (Washington, D.C.; March 20, 1979; 44 Federal Register, 17070–17114).

7. U.S. Atomic Energy Commission [U.S. Nuclear Regulatory Commission], *An Assessment of Accident Risks in U.S. Commercial Nuclear Power Plants* (Washington, D.C., 1974); summary volume AEC Publication WASH-1400 (Aug., 1974). Quoted in William W. Lowrance, *Of Acceptable Risk* (Los Allos: Kaufmann, 1976), p. 73.

8. R. W. Kates, "Hazard and Choice Perception in Flood Plain Management," Research Paper No. 78, Department of Geography, University of Chicago, 1962.

9. J. P. Holdren, "The Nuclear Controversy and the Limitations of Decision Making by Experts," *Bulletin of the Atomic Scientists* 32 (1976): pp. 20–22.

10. G. W. Fairley, "Criteria for Evaluating the 'Small' Probability of a Catastrophic Accident from the Marine Transportation of Liquefied Natural Gas," in *Risk-benefit Methodology and Application: Some Papers Presented at the Engineering Foundation Workshop, Asilomar,* ed. D. Okrent (Los Angeles: University of California, Department of Energy and Kinetics, UCLA-ENG 7598; 1975); Baruch Fischoff, "Cost-benefit Analysis and the Art of Motorcycle Maintenance," *Policy Sciences* 8 (1977): pp. 177–202; A. E. Green and A. J. Bourne, *Reliability Technology* (New York: Wiley-Interscience, 1972); Paul Slovic, "Behavioral Decision Theory," *Annual Review of Psychology* 28 (1977): pp. 1–39; A. Tversky and D. Kahneman, "Judgment under Uncertainty: Heuristics and Biases," *Science* 185 (1974): pp. 1124–31.

11. See Kenneth J. Arrow, "Alternative Approaches to the Theory of Choice in Risk-Taking Situations," *Econometrica* 19 (1951): pp. 404–37 (see. p. 414).

12. Bernoulli's original 1730 essay, "Specimen theoriae novae de mensura sortis," is translated into German by A. Pringsheim as *Versuch einer neuen Theorie von Glücksfällen* (Leipzig, 1896).

13. See Richard Jeffrey, *The Logic of Decision*, 2d ed. (Chicago and London: University of Chicago Press, 1983), pp. 151–55. The classical approach of Bernoulli himself was to conduct the evaluative process in terms of utility rather than money, envisioning the utility of money to decline exponentially with amount. Another approach is to deploy Herbert Simon's conception of satisfying with its view that "enough is enough." See Michael A. Slote, *Beyond Optimizing* (Cambridge, Mass.: Harvard University Press, 1989).

14. It is also possible to entertain the idea of utter catastrophes conceived of as "unacceptable" possibilities that one would not be prepared to risk under any circumstances—no matter how small the possibility of their realization. But this poses different issues and leads into other directions than those presently in view.

15. On the opposite side of the coin lies the distinction between mere disasters and outright catastrophes—the latter being eventuations so horrendous that we would in no circumstances accept any course of action that involves a probability of realization

greater than genuine zero. On this issue see the author's *Risk* (Lanham, Md.: University Press of America, 1983), pp. 75–76.

16. The German proverb has it that "Kleinvieh macht auch Mist." More seriously, a wide spectrum of trivially small risks can become collectively nontrivial, which is why people go to Lloyds for insurance.

17. This proviso will require setting the boundaries for what is to be a single decision context. But this issue, while not without its difficulties, involves ultimately manageable complexities that lead beyond the limits of the present deliberations.

*Chapter 7*

# Nomic Hierarchies
# and Problems of Relativism

## 1. NOMIC HIERARCHIES

The idea of a nomic hierarchy—a hierarchy of principles and values—is a virtually indispensable instrument of rational deliberation. Such a "cultivation hierarchy" (as one may call it) characterizes any purposively oriented human endeavor. It takes the generic format:

- Determinate "finalities": the characterizing aims of the enterprise
- Governing principles that define the specific bearing of these broad orientations
- Guiding norms, criteria, and standards delineating the basic values and desiderata at work in implementing policies
- Methods of procedure (operating rules)
- Specific rulings

The top-level purpose is itself "ultimate" for its own domain: it defines and specifies what is at issue in the venture under consideration, the concerns that make it the sort of project it is (be it science or horticulture). And the successive descending levels each address the matter of implementing the previously fixed aims and objectives.

Justification at each successively more subordinate level is thus purposive and turns on questions of efficiency and effectiveness in serving the needs of the next, superordinated higher level. There is a step-by-step descent from finalities (the characteristic aims inherent in the very definition of valid, need-meeting enterprises) through norms to rules and eventually to specific rulings. And it should be stressed that all of these stages of rationale development appertain equally to the realms of rational belief, action, and evaluation. The same story holds for any inherently goal-oriented human project—medicine or dietetics or science or whatever. In every case, such a hierarchical series descends from the overarching defining objective of the enterprise at issue down to the specific resolutions of concrete cases. The same structure of practical reasoning by subordination under higher-level norms obtains throughout.

Take medicine for example. The cultivation hierarchy at issue here runs along the following lines:

1. *Finalities*: Aims of the enterprise. "Maintaining health."
2. *Governing Principles*: "Curing illness and disease," "restoring and maintaining normal bodily functioning," "removing painful symptoms." (Note that if *these* things are not at issue, then *medicine* is not at issue. An enterprise not concerned with any of these, whatever it may be, is not medicine.)
3. *Governing norms, standards, and criteria*: "How is one to assess 'health'?" "How is one to construe a satisfactory 'normality'?" "How is one to identify a 'symptom'?" "Just what constitutes an 'illness'?" (Note that for the Greeks, unlike ourselves, the idea of an illness without subject-experienced symptoms was scarcely conceivable. At this level there is already some room for variation.)
4. *Rules of procedure*: the modus operandi of medical practices—surgery or chiropractic treatment, drugs or psychotherapy, and the like. (These of course differ drastically from age to age and culture to culture.)
5. *Rationally warranted rulings*: the particular interventions, prescriptions, and medical measures adopted in particular cases. ("Take two aspirin and get some rest.")

The nomic hierarchy of this sort leads from a fixed "top level" characterizing aim, health, through governing norms and values (like "well-nourished," "well-rested," "mentally balanced") to particular rules ("Eat and drink adequately," "Get enough rest"; etc.). Finally, we move via moderating injunctions ("Three meals a day") down to the particular decisions and rulings of medical practice (particular diet plans or prescriptions). The top levels of such a normative hierarchy are "ultimate"—they define and specify what is at issue in the venture under consideration in its nature and implications. Here we deal with such universals.

At the top level there is a fixity and uniformity based in conceptual constraints inherent in the very definition of the nature of the enterprise. But uniformity is achieved here at the price of an abstractness and generality that endows the principles at issue with a conditional or hypothetical character. As we move downward toward the level of particular cases, the situation is increasingly one of concrete detail, and this detail brings increasing scope for variation in its wake. Thus, while the top level is itself absolute and constant, there is "slack" at each step down the ladder, leaving (appropriate) room for an increasingly large element of variability and differentiation. At each successive step in the process of subordination there is some degree of underdetermination—scope for diversity and some degree of contextual variability. (In the cognitive case, variability arises with such issues as: What sorts of rules best implement the demands for cogent deductive and inductive reasoning? What sorts of solutions do schematic rules such as "Adapt theories to the data as well as possible" lead to?) As we move down this hierarchic ladder there emerges an increasing looseness of fit that provides for the differential adaptation of general principles to the specific characteristics of particular settings and circumstances.

In the medical case, for example, we get such norms as: maintaining health, and more specifically, maintaining health through nourishment (eating), and more specifically, getting nourishment by eating healthy foods that one also happens to like. Observe, however, that all of these more specific implementation formula are also *universally* appropriate modes of operation: Doing the things involved is rational for *everybody*. But this universality becomes increasingly qualified in its conditions of application when one proceeds down the ladder by appropriate steps.[1] (Clearly, not everyone happens to like meat in general or steak in particular.) And so, there is much room for variation in the concrete implementation of universals. As regards (level 2), different things are nourishing for different people, given their particular biomedical makeup. And as regards (level 3) it is clear that different people like different things.

How a principle such as "Do not drive in a way that needlessly endangers the lives of others" gets implemented will depend on a great many factors of situational variation (weather conditions, visibility conditions, the expectations of others as defined by local speed limits, and on and on). As one moves through the lower levels of such a hierarchy, there is a "slack" that leaves room for increasing variability and dissensus. Specific rules and guidelines will vary with situations and circumstances—different experiential contexts. "Maintaining an alert mind" is in *everyone's* medical interest, but "getting eight hours regular sleep" is appropriate only for some.

For a particular normative resolution to qualify as rationally valid, the entire ascending chain of subordination that links it to those topmost determinative finalities must thus be appropriately validated. The whole rationale developed in terms of such a cultivation hierarchy must be cogent "all the way up" for the ruling itself to be rationally cogent. If there is not a filiation of continuity—if a particular measure is not part of a long story that leads from our concrete choices all the way up to that fixed and stable top level of the principles that define "the aims of the (in the present case *medical*) enterprise"—then it is really not a genuine *medical* measure that is in question. Throughout, justification of one's proceedings at lower levels involves an appeal to the higher. But the highest level is final in its defining role for the overall enterprise at issue. (After all, medicine—or cognition—is a definite sort of enterprise, different in its teleological nature from ventures such as butterfly collecting.)

The situation in medicine as we have depicted it here is mirrored in a very different areas as well. Take that of warfare. Here too we have a nomically geared cultivation hierarchy—one that, in this case, has the following format:

1. Ultimate aims: bending a group's enemies to its will by the use of fire
2. Strategic principles
3. Tactical rules (the guiding precepts of Jomini and Clausewitz versus tactical manuals)
4. Operating procedures (regulations, standard practices)
5. Specific orders and directions

As one moves down this list, there is an ongoing diminution in the range of generality and validity of what is at issue, with diminishing abstractness resulting in an increase in concrete specificity.

Such a normative hierarchy of rationale-furnishing levels always plays a crucial role in providing for the rational legitimation of what we do. At its pinnacle there is some rationally valid (appropriately interest-serving) desideratum such as health (or rationality itself) to furnish the "ultimate" pivot point, but moving down the line we encounter the increasingly more concrete factors of rationalization, until ultimately we arrive at specific determinations about concrete items. Here, there is increasing room for context-supplied development, variation, and dissensus.

In such an "implementation hierarchy" we thus descend from what is abstractly and fixedly universal to what is concrete and variable. Level 2 is contained in level 1 simply by way of exfoliative "explication." But as we move downward past level 3 to the implementing specifications of level 4, there is—increasingly—a looseness or "slack" that makes room for the specific and variable ways of different groups for implementing the particular higher-level objective at issue.

## 2. THE CASE OF RATIONALITY

Let us now turn to the idea of rationality. How can the absolutistic universality of the defining principles of rationality—themselves rooted in the monolithic uniformity of "what rationality is"—possibly be reconciled with

1. *Defining aims of rationality.* The basic principles that determine the nature of the enterprise and specify what rationality is all about. (For cognitive rationality, for example, the project at issue turns on the pursuit of truth and the achievement of correct answers to our questions: "The truth, the whole truth, and nothing but the truth.")

2. *Basic principles.* Ruling principles provide our criteria for assessing the acceptability and adequacy of rational norms and standards of rational procedure.

3. *Governing norms and standards of rationality.* Standards for appraising the "rules of the game" governing the rational transaction of affairs. (For cognitive rationality, these norms are afforded by desiderata such as coherence, consistency, simplicity, and the like.) These norms provide our criteria for assessing the acceptability and adequacy of our rules of rational procedure.

4. *Rules of rational procedure.* Rules for the rational resolution of choices. (In the cognitive case, rules such as *modus ponens* in deductive inference or trend extrapolation in inductive inference.) These rules constitute our criteria for assessing the rational acceptability and adequacy of particular resolutions.

5. *Rationally warranted rulings.* Resolutions with respect to particular issues arising in particular concrete cases, such as: "Do (or accept) *X* in the existing circumstances."

**Figure 7.1.   Stratification Levels of Principles of Rationality**

the pluralistic diversity of appropriate answers to the question: "What is it rational to do?" The answer lies in the fact that various intermediate levels, or strata, of consideration separate these abstract and uniform "basic principles of rationality" from concrete resolutions about what it is rational to do in the variegated plurality of particular circumstances and conditions that prevail in the world. The tabulation of figure 7.1 depicts this descending hierarchy of principles, norms and standards, rules, and (finally) rulings, which comprises the structure of rationale development. There is a distinctive hierarchical continuum of levels throughout. At the top of the hierarchy, the defining principles of rationality specify the characterizing aims of the enterprise. They explicate what is at issue: the giving of good reasons for what we do, the provision of a reasonable account, the telling of a sensible story (*lógon didónai, rationem reddere*). The characteristic mission of rationality is that of providing an account of our dealings, of committing ourselves in the context of our affairs to "making sense," of rendering our dealings intelligible, of conducting our affairs intelligently. At the next level down, the governing norms and standards are our yardsticks of rational procedure: basic principles of logic, canons of inductive reasoning, standards of evidence, and the like, which already admit of some variation. Then, descending further, we encounter the "rules of the game" that specify the procedures through which we implement ends and objectives of the enterprise in the concrete context of particular cases. Finally, at the bottom level, come the specific resolutions for particular cases achieved through the subsumption of concrete cases under the rules. (It is clearly these last that vary most of all.)

Accordingly, in being rational, we pursue universal desiderata in person-differential ways—ways that we have good reason to deem effective in the peculiar conditions of our particular case. Not all of us eat what Tom does. But we can, all of us, (1) explain and understand his eating kumquats once we realize that he happens to like them and (responsibly) believes them to be both hunger removing and healthful, and (2) agree that the modus operandi involved in his case ("eating what one likes and responsibly believes to be nourishing") is one to which we ourselves do (and should) subscribe. Rationality is a matter of pursuing valid (and universally appropriate) desiderata as ends by appropriate means (but means that are *individually* appropriate and adjusted to the circumstances of one's personal situation).[2]

This perspective makes it clear that a uniformitarian absolutism at the top level of "what rationality is" is perfectly consonant with a pluralism and relativism at the ground level of concrete resolutions regarding "what is rational" in particular cases.[3] The ruling principles of rationality never uniquely constrain their more specific implementations; their application to concrete circumstances always permits some degree of "slack." At each step along the way we repeat the same basic situation: delimitation, yes; determination, no. Resolutions can, in principle, always be accomplished in distinct yet still appropriate ways. The sought-for reconciliation between the universalistic absoluteness of rationality and the variability and relativity of its particular rulings is thus provided by the consideration that the absolutism of principles operates at the highest level of the hierarchy of rationale development, while there is ever more "slack" and variability as one moves toward the lowest level of concrete determinations. The variability and relativity of good reasons at the level of our actual operations can indeed be reconciled with the absolutism of rationality itself by taking a hierarchical view of the process through which the absolutistic conception of ideal rationality is brought to bear on the resolution of concrete cases and particular situations.[4]

## 3. THE CASE OF MORALITY

Morality is also a purposive human project—one whose cohesive unity as such resides in its functional objective of molding the behavior of people through a care for one another's interests. Accordingly, we here again have an implementation hierarchy. We at once move to deal with a descending sequence of characterizing aims, fundamental principles and values, governing rules, implementing directives, and (finally) particular rulings. (See figure 7.2.)

At the topmost level we have the defining aims and objectives of the moral enterprise as such by specifying what morality is all about—namely, acting

Level 1: *Characterizing Aims of the Enterprise*

- To support the best interests of people and to avoid injuring them

Level 2: *Basic Principles (Controlling Values)*

- Do not cause people needless pain (GENTLENESS)
- Do not endanger people's lives or their well-being unnecessarily (CARE FOR SAFETY)
- Honor your genuine commitments to people; in dealing with people give them their just due (PROBITY)
- Help others when you reasonably can (GENEROSITY)
- Don't take improper advantage of others(FAIRNESS)

Level 3: *Operating Rules*

- Don't hurt people unnecessarily
- Don't lie; don't say what you believe not to be so
- Don't cheat

Level 4: *Operating Directives*

- Be candid when replying to appropriate questions
- Do not play with unfair dice
- Where possible use anesthetics when operating on people

Level 5: *Concrete Rulings*

- Return the money you borrowed from Smith
- Don't pollute this river; dispose of your sewage elsewhere
- Don't let these children play with those matches

**Figure 7.2. Illustrations from the Implementation Hierarchy of Morality**

with a view to safeguarding the valid interests of others. These characterizing aims of morality represent the overarching "defining objectives" that delineate the project as such. They explicate what is at issue when it is with *morality*— rather than, say, basket weaving—that we propose to concern ourselves. In spelling out the fundamental idea of what morality is all about, these top-level norms provide the ultimate reference points of moral deliberation. And they are unalterably fixed—inherent in the very nature of the subject.

And these fundamental "aims of the enterprise" also fix the basic principles and controlling values that delineate the moral virtues (honesty, trustworthiness, civility, probity, and the rest). Such values define the salient norms that link the abstract characterizing aims to an operational morality of specific governing rules. The norms embodied in these basic principles and values are "universal" and "absolute" features of morality, inherent in the enterprise and serving as parts of what makes morality the thing it is. (Examples: "Do not violate the duly established rights and claims of others." "Do not unjustly deprive others of life, liberty, or opportunity for self-development." "Do not tell self-serving false-hoods." "Do not deliberately aid and abet others in wrongdoing.") Accordingly these high-level principles also lie fixedly in the very nature of the subject. At these two topmost levels, then, there is accordingly no room for any "disagreement about morality." Here disagreement betokens misunderstanding: if one does not recognize the fundamental aims, principles, and values that characterize the moral enterprise as such, then one is simply dealing with something else altogether. In any discussion of *morality* these things are fixed givens.

However, this situation changes as one moves further down the list and takes additional steps in the descent to concreteness. Thus at the next (third) level we encounter the governing rules and regulations that direct the specifically moral transaction of affairs. Here we have the generalities of the usual and accustomed sort: "Do not lie," "Do not cheat," "Do not steal," etc. At this level we come to the imperatives that guide our deliberations and decisions. Like the Ten Commandments, they set out the controlling dos and don'ts of the moral practice of a community, providing us with general guidance in moral conduct. Already here variability begins to set in. These rules implement morality's ruling principles at the concrete level of recommended practices in a way that admits of adjustment to the changeable circumstances of local conditions. A generalized moral rule on the order of the injunction

Do not steal! = Do not take something that properly belongs to another!

is something abstract and schematic. It requires the concrete fleshing out of substantive implementing specifications to tell us what sorts of things make for "proper ownership."

And so the next (fourth) level presents us with the ground rules of procedure or implementing directives that furnish our working guidelines and criteria for the moral resolution of various types of cases. (Example: "Killing is wrong except in cases of self-defense or under legal mandate as in war or executions.") At this level of implementing standards and criteria, the variability of local practice comes to the fore, so that there is further room for pluralistic diversification here; we ourselves implement "Do not lie, avoid telling falsehoods," by way of "Say what you believe (to be the case)," but a society of convinced skeptics could not do so. The operating ground rules of level four accordingly incorporate the situation-relative standards and criteria though which the more abstract, higher-level rules get their grip on concrete situations. Those general rules themselves are too abstract—too loose or general to be applicable without further directions to give them a purchase on concrete situations. They must be given concrete implementation with reference to local—and thus variable—arrangements.[5]

Finally, at the lowest (fifth) level we came to the particular moral rulings, individual resolutions with respect to the specific issues arising in concrete cases. (Example: "It was wicked of Lady Macbeth to incite her husband to kill the king.") Attunement to the variable additions of concrete contexts is the order of the day here.

The entire hierarchy comes to a head in a ruling imperative ("Support the interests of people!") that stands correlative with an enterprise-determinative value ("the best interests of people"). This overarching concern does not itself stand subordinate to further moral rules. After all, it is only possible up to a certain point that we can have rules for applying rules and principles for applying principles. The process of validating lower-level considerations in terms of higher-level ones must come to a stop somewhere. And with these implementation hierarchies it is the overarching controlling teleology of "the aim of the entire enterprise" that gives at once unity and determinatives to the justificatory venture.

## 4. MORAL ABSOLUTES AND THE HIERARCHY-INDUCED OBJECTION TO MORAL RELATIVISM

Even as there are many ways to build houses, fuel automobiles, or skin cats, so there are various ways of being moral. But this does explicitly not mean that there is no overarching unity of goals, functions, principles, and values to lend a definitional cohesion to the enterprise. Moral variability is more apparent than real—an absolute uniformity does, and must, prevail at the level of fundamentals. "Act with due heed of the interests of others" is a universal and absolute moral principle whose working out in different contexts will, to be sure, very much depend on just exactly how the interests of people happen to be reciprocally intertwined. But despite the diversity of the substantive moral codes of different societies, the basic overarching principles of morality are uniform and invariant—inherent in the very idea of what morality is all about. Here too we have a nomic hierarchy whose topmost level is determinative.

Viewed from this perspective it emerges that different "moralities" are simply diverse implementations of certain uniform, overarching moral *principles*. There is ample room for situational variation and pluralism in response to the question: "What is the morally appropriate thing to do?" But there is no such room with respect to: "What is morality—and what are the principles at issue here?" The concept of morality and its contents are fixed by the "*questioner's prerogative*" inherent in the principle that it is the inquirer's own conception of the matter that is determinative for what is at issue in his inquiries.

In *our deliberations* about moral rights and wrongs it is thus *our conception* of "morality" and its governing principles that is conclusive for what is at issue. When *we* engage in deliberations about morality—be it our own or that of others—it is "morality" *as we understand it* that figures in this discussion.[6] And this circumstance of theoretic fixity engenders a fixity of those project-definitive moral principles.

All modes of morality have important elements in common simply in view of the fact that *morality* is at issue. Since (by hypothesis) they all qualify as "modes of morality," they are bound to encompass such fundamental considerations as:

- What people do matters. Some actions are right, others wrong, some acceptable and some not. There is an important difference here.
- This is not just a matter of convention, custom, and the done thing. Violations of moral principles are not just offenses against sensibility but against people's just claims in matters where people's actual well-being is at stake.
- In violating the moral rules we inflict injury on the life, welfare, or otherwise legitimate interests of others—either actually or by way of putting them unjustifiedly at risk.

Attunement to consideration of this sort is *by definition* essential to any system of "morality," and serves to provide the basis for imperatives such as:

- Do not simply ignore other people's rights and claims in your own deliberations!
- Do not inflict needless pain on people!
- Honor the legitimate interests of others!
- Do not take what rightfully belongs to others without their appropriately secured consent!
- Do not wantonly break promises!
- Do not cause someone anguish simply for your own amusement!

In the context of *morality*, principles and rules of this sort are universal and absolute. They are of the very essence of morality; in abandoning them we would withdraw from a discussion of *morality* and would, in effect, be changing the subject. What we say might be interesting—and even true—but it would deal with another topic.

"But how can you pivot the issue on 'the very idea of what "morality" is all about'? After all, different people have different ideas about this." Of course different people think differently about morality, even as they think differently about dogs or automobiles. But that is basically irrelevant. What is at issue with "morality" as such does not lie with you or with me but with all of us. What is relevantly at issue is how the word is actually used in the community—in the linguistic culture in which our discussion of the issue transpires. It is a matter not of what people think about the topic, but of how they use the terminology that defines it.

Yet, how can this fixity of the conception of morality and of the basic principles that are at issue within it—inherent in the monolithic uniformity of "what *morality* is"—be reconciled with the plain fact of a pluralistic diversity of (presumably cogent) answers to the question: "What is it moral to do?" How can such an absolutism of morality's fundamentals coexist with the patent relativity of moral evaluations across different times and cultures?

The answer lies in the fact that several intermediate levels or strata inevitably separate those overarching "basic principles of morality" from any concrete judgments about what it is moral to do.

Overall, then, we have to deal with a chain of subordination likages that connect a concrete moral judgment—a particular moral act-recommendation or command—with the ultimate defining aim of the moral enterprise. The long and short of it is that any appropriate moral injunction must derive its validity through being an appropriate instantiation or concretization of an overarching principle of universal (unrestricted) validity under which it is subsumed. It must, in short, represent a circumstantially appropriate implementation of the fixities of absolute morality. Thus, even as in Roman Catholic theology there is a "hierarchy of truths" that places different teachings of the church at different levels of doctrinal essentiality or fundamentality, so in the present context there is a comparable hierarchy of imperatival strata that place different injunctions at different levels of fundamentality in the moral enterprise, with some (the basic principles) as, in this setting, absolute, and others as variable and relative to context and circumstance. Fundamentals are fixed as essential to the domain as such, but agreement on concrete issues is itself something more marginal.

The crucial fact is that one selfsame moral value—fairness, for example—can come into operation very differently in different contexts. In an economy of abundance it may militate for equality of shares, in an economy of scarcity for equality of opportunity. The particular circumstances that characterize a context of operation may importantly condition the way in which a moral value or principle can (appropriately) be applied. We cannot expect to encounter any universal consensus across cultural and temporal divides: physicians of different eras are (like moralists) bound to differ—and to some extent those of different cultures as well. There is—inevitably—substantial variability among particular groups, each with its own varying ideas conditioned by locally prevailing conditions and circumstances. But the impact of low-level variation is mitigated by the fact that justification at lower levels proceeds throughout with reference to superordinated standards in a way that makes for higher-level uniformity. Uniform high-level principles will have to be implemented differently in different circumstances. Medicine and morality alike are complex projects unified and integrated amidst the welter of changing conditions and circumstances by the determinative predominance of high-level principles.

At the level of basic principles, then, morality is absolute; its strictures at this level hold good for everyone, for all rational agents. And lower-level rules and rulings must—if valid—preserve a "linkage of subsumption" to those highest-level abstractions, a linkage mediated by way of more restrictive modes of implementation. These implementing rules involve contextual relativity—coordination with contingently variable (setting-dependent and era- and culture-variable) circumstances and situations. Thus, while moral objectives and basic principles—those top levels of the hierarchy of moral norms—are absolute and universal, "slack" arises as we move further down the ladder, leaving room for (quite appropriate) contextual variability and differentiation. "Do not unjustifiably take the property of another for your own use" is an unquestionably valid principle of absolute morality. But it avails nothing until such time as there are means for determining what is "the property of another" and what constitutes "unjustified taking." "Don't break promises merely for your own convenience" is a universal moral rule, and as such is global and absolute. But what sorts of practices constitute making a valid promise is something that is largely determined through localized social conventions. Local context—variable history, tradition, expectation-defining legal systems, and the like—thus makes for substantial variability at the level of operational rules and codes, of moral practices.

From the moral point of view, the *empirical* search for "cultural invariants" as pursued by some ethnologists is thus entirely beside the point.[7] When such investigations embark on a cross-cultural quest for "moral universals" or "universal values" amidst the variation of social customs, they are engaged in a search that, however interesting and instructive in its own way, has nothing whatever to do with the sort of normative universality at issue with morality as such. Moral universality is not a matter of cross-cultural commonality but of a *conceptually* constrained uniformity. (It would be just as pointless to investigate whether another culture's forks have tynes.) The variability of *mores* makes only a limited impact upon the uniformitarian absolutism of *morals*.

## 5. AGAINST MORAL RELATIVISM

The long and short of it is that the anthropological reduction of morality to mores just does not work. Some things are wrong in an absolute and universal way:

- Killing another person for reasons of revenge
- Taking improper advantage of people
- Inflicting pointless harm
- Lying and deception for selfish advantage, betraying a trust for personal gain
- Breaking promises out of sheer perversity
- Misusing the institutions of one's society for one's own purposes

The unacceptability (i.e., moral inappropriateness) of such actions lies in the very idea of what morality is all about. Local custom to the contrary notwithstanding, such things are morally wrong anytime, anywhere, and for anyone. Their prohibitions are moral universals—parts of morality as such. (And so they hold good not just for us humans but for all rational beings.)

To be sure, different societies operate with different moral ground rules at the procedural level. Some societies deem it outrageous for women to expose their faces, their breasts, their knees; others view this as altogether acceptable and perhaps even mandatory. But behind this variation stands a universal principle: "Respect people's sensibilities about the appropriate and acceptable appearance of fellow humans by conforming to established rules of proper modesty." This overarching principle is universal and absolute. Its implementation with respect to, say, elbows or belly buttons is of course something that varies with custom and the practices of the community. The rule itself is abstract and schematic—in need of implementing criteria as to what "proper modesty" demands. The matter is one of a universal principle with variable implementations subject to locally established standards and criteria that are grounded in the particular customs of the community.

At the level of fundamentals the variability of moral codes is underpinned by an absolute uniformity of moral principles and values. At the highest levels alone is there absoluteness: here an impersonal cogency of acceptance prevails—the rejection of appropriate contentions at this level involves a lapse of rational cogency. But at the lower levels there is almost always some room for variation—and dispute as well. (How concern for the well-being of one's fellows can be brought to effective expression, for example, will very much depend on the institutions of one's society—and also, to some extent, on one's place within it.)

But what we have here is a contextualism of local appropriateness that is something very different from a relativism of universal indifference—"Ultimately it does not matter; to each his own; it is just a matter of custom; morality is not more than mores."

And so, the looseness of fit or "slack" that we encounter increasingly as we move toward that bottom level of concreteness makes for considerable context-specific variability at that bottom level. Here underdetermination may come into play through the existence of plausible reasons for divergent positions without any prospect of categorical resolution one way or the other. A situation of moral indeterminacy may arise where each one of several equally cogent positions can come into irreconcilable conflict. The same respect for life that leads one person to take up arms against a tyrant may lead another to walk in the path of pacifism and self-sacrifice. Either position is defensible and both deserve moral recognition and respect: in a dispute between these two variant appraisals there is no single unique right answer. In settings of scarcity (battlefield triage situations, for example) there may well be very real morally laden choices—relieve suffering versus promote survival, for instance—where there is no definitive right or wrong.[8]

But a definite linkage of subordination and coordination is maintained throughout the implementation process. The validity of concrete rulings is always a matter of their attuning global (and abstract) prescriptions to local (and concrete) conditions. Without that linkage to the fixed highest-level absolutes, the linkage to morality is severed. For a particular ruling to be a proper moral ruling at all, there must be a suitable moral *rationale* for the action—a pathway of subordination linkages that connects it in a continuous manner all the way up to the characterizing aims of the moral enterprise. Varying practices and codes of procedure only possess moral validity insofar as they are implementations of a fixed and determinate set of moral principles. Moral validity must always root in a moral universality that is constrained by a *conceptual* fixity.

Morality's characteristic universality is thus inevitably mediated through factors that are variable, conventional, and culturally relative. That project-definitive general principle must be implemented in concrete circumstances and be adapted to them, even as the idea of hospitality toward strangers, for example, has to function differently in European and in Bedouin cultures, seeing that deserts and cities are very different human environments. Still, the deeper moral principles that underlie the moral rules and practices of a society ("Even strangers have their due—they too are entitled to respect, to courtesy, and to assistance in need") transcend the customs of any particular community. As concerns morality, culture is indeed a localizing and differentiating agent—but one that merely conditions to local circumstances those fundamental invariants that are inherent in the very conception of morality as such.

The local "moralities" of various communities merely canalize and implement such general principles in a way that attunes them to the character of local conditions and circumstances. For the universality of fundamental moral principles does *not* mean that all moral agents must proceed in exactly the same way at the level of concrete detail. (To revert to the preceding example: medical competence too is also based on uniform and universal principles—

conscientious care to provide the best available treatment for one's patients; but that does not mean that competent doctors must in all times, places, and circumstances administer the same treatments.)

And so, while the concrete strictures of morality—its specific ordinances and procedural rules of thumb—will of course differ from age to age and culture to culture, nevertheless the ultimate principles that serve to define the project of "morality" as such are universal. The uniform governing conception of "what morality is" suffices to establish and standardize those ultimate and fixed principles that govern the moral enterprise as such. At the top of that nomic hierarchy we have a condition of uniform fixity that is nowise at odds with situational and contextual variability at the lower levels.

## NOTES

This essay was initially published in Mattias Gutman et. al. (eds.), *Kultur-Handlung-Wissenschaft* ed. Mattias Gutman et al. (Weiderwest: Velbrick Wissenschart, 2002), pp. 285–301. Reprinted by kind permission of the publisher.

1. Note that it is not homogeneously a means–end hierarchy. (Steak is not a *means* to food; it is a *kind* of food.)

2. It sounds circular to say that rationality consists in pursuing valid ends by appropriate means, seeing that rationality itself will have to be the arbiter of validity and appropriateness. But *this* sort of "circularity" is virtuous and not vicious.

3. Note that this comes to "what rationality *as we understand it* is."

4. Note, too, that different top-level finalities can lead to priority conflicts through competing demands on resources. Health and knowledge, or family life and professional life, for example, may certainly conflict—not, to be sure, as abstract desiderata but in the competing demands that arise in the course of their practical implementation. Insofar as such conflicts are rationally resolvable at all, still other finalities must be involved as arbiters. Even at the highest levels, our valid aims are not really "ultimate"—save for in their own domains.

5. The analogy of natural law is helpful: "Theft, murder, adultery and all injuries are forbidden by the laws of nature; but which is to be called theft, what murder, what adultery, what injury in a citizen, this is not to be determined by the natural but by the civil law" (Thomas Hobbes, *De Cive*, chap. IV, sect. 16). St. Thomas holds that appropriate human law must be subordinate to the natural law by way of "particular determination"; with different human laws, varying from place to place, nevertheless representing appropriate concretizations of the same underlying principle of natural law. (See *Summa Theologica*, IaIIae, questions 95–96.)

6. But just who are the "we" at issue? Clearly, those who are members of our linguistic community—those who realize that when we speak of "morality" we mean *morality* (with the various things involved therein), and not, say, basket weaving.

7. See Clyde Kluckhohn, *Culture and Behavior* (Glencoe, Ill.: The Free Press, 1962); Kluckholm, "Ethical Relativity; Sic et Non," *The Journal of Philosophy* 52 (1955): 663–77; R. Redfield, "The Universally Human and the Culturally Variable," *The Journal of General Education* 10 (1967): 150–60; Ralph Linton, "Universal Ethical Principles: An Anthropological View," in R. N. Anshen (ed.), *Moral Principles of Action*, ed. R. F. Spencer (New York: Free Press, 1952); Linton, "The Problem of Universal Values," in *Method and Perspective in Anthropology*, ed. R. F. Spencer (Minneapolis: University of Minnesota Press, 1954).

8. Aspects of these issues are helpfully discussed in Susan Wolf, "Two Levels of Pluralism," *Ethics* 102 (1992): pp. 785–98.

*Part Two*

# PUBLIC POLICY ISSUES

# Chapter Eight

# Technology, Complexity, and Social Decision

## 1. TECHNOLOGICAL PROGRESS MAKES LIFE MORE COMPLICATED

We members of *Homo sapiens* are amphibious creatures: we inhabit two spheres, the realm of nature and the realm of human artifice. The former domain is one where we *find* matters in place; the latter is a *construct* that we ourselves produce under the guidance of intelligence. But on both sides alike we encounter an unfathomable complexity. Nature has levels of depth extending beyond any point that our cognitive efforts can manage to attain, and human artifice also carries us ever further down the road of complexification. And this ever-increasing complexity makes it ongoingly difficult to manage our affairs not only in matters of thought but in matters of decision and action as well. It is both instructive and constructive to consider the reasons and consequences of this state of things.

Biological evolution under the aegis of natural selection makes for ever more specialized speciation, differentially selecting for those organisms who branch off toward a particular variety able to respond more effectively to the challenges of changing environmental conditions. Biological evolution accordingly makes for increasingly complex organisms.

And technological evolution has exactly the same tendency. In virtually every sphere of our human concerns we constantly encounter new obstacles. And new problems call for doing what we were unable to do before; they require new solutions that themselves call for new methods, new processes, new instrumentalities. Such escalating demands stimulate technical progress. We are driven to devising more complex systems that put increasing performative sophistication at our disposal. We here encounter the fundamental Law of Technical Progress: *Human artifice is caught up in a complexity tropism*. And the rationale of this situation is easy to understand on principles of economy of effort, seeing that rational creatures are naturally inclined to try simpler solutions first, maintaining them until such time as it becomes advantageous to replace them by something more complicated. In consequence, all of our creative efforts—in material, social, and intellectual contexts alike—manifest a historical tendency moving from the simpler to the more complex.

We are generally inclined to think that technological progress makes life easier. But the fact is that technological progress makes life vastly more complicated by widening the range of choice and opportunity, thereby increasing the operational complexity of process all about us. Technological progress helps in detail but always complicates matters in the large by posing new challenges to decision.

Anyone who is tempted to think that technology makes things simpler as it makes things better should compare a Ford Model T with its contemporary successor. We pay for the advantages of sophisticated technology by confronting issues of operational choice and decision that are of ever increasing complexity. The complexities of information management and control in technologically sophisticated settings pose enormous demands. As technology advances, the problems of cognitive discrimination—just like those of visual discrimination—expand exponentially in line with the proliferation of possibilities.[1] And so, while technological progress—be it material or social—may indeed facilitate and ease the performance of particular tasks, its aggregate effect is to make large-scale processes more complicated.

In the course of scientific and technical progress, the management of complexity calls for ever greater sophistication, and thus in turn imposes problems of decision in the face of exploding information. The driver of a horse and buggy can afford to doze off, but the driver of a car can afford it far less, and the pilot of a supersonic fighter plane not at all. With more sophisticated camera equipment one will always need to make many more detailed decisions about locating the optimal perspectives from which to take a picture. And if we replace these human decision makers with automatic control devices, each must be many orders of magnitude more complex and sophisticated than its more rudimentary compeers. The problem of complexity management is now simply shifted from one of operating a system to one of managing the functioning of its cybernetic governance. The drug industry is subject to far more regulations today than the entire economy was fifty years ago. In combat, the pilot of a jet fighter makes far more operational decisions in five minutes than a sailing-era ship's captain did in a day.[2]

But what of a "return to the past"—a nostalgia-satisfying reversion to the conditions of an earlier, simpler age? The short answer is that this is simply impracticable outside the limited range of museum-piece environments in isolated backwaters. We would not have resorted to those complications in the first place if we had not been forced to them by the needs of the situation. In general, the price of a return is unaffordable.

To be sure, this is a matter of how things stand in the large and in the whole. It is possible to preserve islands of simplicity in human affairs. But this is possible only in exceptional and highly localized conditions. Overall, the later position in the realm of artifice is bound to be one where complexity is unavoidable and uneliminable.

And so the fact remains that complexity is the inseparable accompaniment of modernity. We encounter it throughout our science, throughout our technology, and throughout our social and cultural environments as well. Perhaps the clearest manifestation of this is the range of choice that confronts us on all sides—with sources of information, means of entertainment and leisure activities, occupations, and even life-styles. An ongoing proliferation in the multiplicity of cultural forms and the diversity of opportunities is a striking and salient feature of our age, and it is an unavoidable feature of what we are pleased to designate as "progress" that it confronts us with an ever more complex and diversified manifold of possibilities. And the obverse scale of such opportunity creation is the matter of *opportunity cost* inherent in the fact that every opportunity we seize also represents a multiplicity of opportunities forgone.

## 2. PROBLEM COMPLEXITY
## OUTPACES SOLUTION COMPLEXITY

Of course, technology is not just part of the problem; it affords part of the solution as well. While technological progress always poses new problems in the management of information and the control of operating procedures, it also of course helps with resolving issues of this sort. Safety engineering in all its forms—redundancy provision, fault detection sensors—together with the "cybernetic" automation of control mechanisms and above all the use of computers in information management and decision implementation all afford powerful resources for problem resolution in technological contexts. Process controls too can be handled in substantial measure by technological means. Interestingly enough, the electronics in a contemporary automobile cost some two thousand dollars more than the steel used to produce the same car.

However, there yet remains the crucial issue of comparative pace. With technological progress, which grows the faster, the manifold of problems to be resolved or the reach and power of our instrumentalities of problem resolution? Now here it might seem that complex technology gives the advantage to problem resolution. After all, do not the cognitive resources that computers provide offset the problems raised by increasing of complexity? Alas, not really.

First, it has to be recognized that computers help principally with information *processing* and do not equally address the problem of information *acquisition*. And in the course of technological progress these become even more extensive and even more significant. Here the classic dictum holds good: as far as the efficacy of computational information manipulation is concerned, garbage in, garbage out. Moreover, the fact remains that computers do just exactly what they are programmed to do. The level of complexity management they are able to achieve is determined through—and thus limited by—the levels of ingenuity and conceptual adequacy of their programming. No central bank places unalloyed confidence in its economic models. And there is also the problem of unforeseen and unforeseeable interactions within the intricacies of the operating processes of computer functioning. These "bugs" can result in malfunctions in computer operation even as they can produce accidents in other sorts of systems. And the more elaborate and complex our programs get—particularly in areas where novelty and innovation are the order of the day—the larger the prospect and chances for such mishaps. Maiden voyages are notoriously fertile in bringing unanticipated difficulties to light.

The fact is that as technical systems become more complex, their operation becomes even more so. And over time managerial complexity generally outpaces the growth of processual sophistication. A more elaborate repertoire always imposes new difficulty in matters of operation and procedure. And, as already noted in chapter 7, process concatenations always grow at a rate faster than the processes themselves.

The long and short of it is that complexity management via computers will not remove the obstacles to managerial effectiveness exactly because complexity raises problems faster than it provides means for their solution. Computers—the very instruments that enhance our capacity for complexity management—widen the scope of the field of action and thereby augment the complexity we face. The technical resources that enlarge our powers in the area of problem resolution not only do not manage to *reduce* the overall size of the problem field that confronts us, but actually manage to *enlarge* it. Technological progress engenders what might be characterized as the "rolling snowball effect" because complexity breeds more complexity through engendering problem situations from which only additional technical capacity can manage to extract us.

With the progress of science, technology, and human artifice generally, complexity is self-potentiating because it engenders complications on the side of problems that can be addressed adequately only through further complication on the side of process and procedure. The increase in technical sophistication confronts us with a dynamic feedback interaction between problems and solutions that ultimately transforms each successive solution into a generator of new problems. And these feedback effects operate in such a way that for all intents and purposes the growth rate of the problem domain continually outpaces that of our capacity to produce solutions. Both our problems and our solutions grow more complex in the wake of technological progress, but the crux of the matter lies in the comparatively greater pace of the increase in problem complexity. The undoubted advantages of modernity are not to be had free of charge.

The gigantism of the managerial machinery of the contemporary city or industrial enterprise or university is thus no accident. Designed for affording greater control over more complex systems, the administrative machine of such organizations is forced to meet even greater challenges in point of performative efficacy. As the functional capacity of such institutions expands under the pressure of technological progress, the scope of management operations expands explosively. With the modern technology of communication and information management, bureaucracy is thus bound to increase irrespective of the particular operational tasks for whose management the bureaucracy is instituted.[3]

## 3. THE INTIMIDATING IMPETUS OF THE UNKNOWN: RISK AND DESTABILIZATION

The growing complexity that emerges in the wake of technical progress always engenders unexpected difficulties. And with every step that we take toward coping with these difficulties, unforeseeable consequences generally arise. All along the line, the Law of Unintended Effects comes into operation. As technical sophistication increases, we penetrate ever further into a domain where we cannot see clearly along the road that lies ahead. We continually confront problem situations within which not only can we not determine *optimal* solutions, but where even the identification of *desirable* solutions becomes problematic and imponderable.

This phenomenon has ominous implications. *Physical chaos*, it will be recalled, occurs when a system functions in so volatile a way that a minute difference in its initial condition—a difference so small as to lie beneath the threshold of observation and perhaps even of observability—can make for a vast difference for the state that ensues. *Cognitive chaos* is exactly the same sort of thing transposed to the region of information processing. It occurs whenever a minute variation in input information can produce great difference in its inferential consequences—that is, whenever an inferential outcome is enormously sensitive to small variations in informational input. The prospect of subjecting such processes to adequate cognitive control by way of principled understanding is somewhere between small and nonexistent. And it is just here that complexity makes itself felt.

As systems grow increasingly complex, they become more difficult to control, both intellectually and physically. The prospect of insufficient or misleading information grows along with system complexity and, other things equal, sophisticated systems need to have more elaborate processes. Prediction too becomes less practicable, save at the level of statistical indefiniteness. The activities of a primitive tribe are easier to predict than those of the U.S. Congress; extra-heavy atoms are less stable than extra-light ones; strategy is easier to manage with tic-tac-toe than with chess. Screws are more complex than nails, but thereby more limited. They do a better job at holding things together, but are less versatile (all sorts of things can be nailed together while screws require a porous material such as wood). The general structure of the situation is reflected in the circumstance that while simple systems are more versatile and flexible but less effective and efficient; complex systems are more specialized but less adaptable. Complex systems pay for greater efficiency and effectiveness through being more specialized, more closely attuned to the circumstantial specifics of the case. They are, accordingly, easier to destabilize—more vulnerable to the interventions of chaos.

As the operations of a goal-directed system of any sort become more complex, there increasingly comes to the fore the importance of safety engineering—of devising contrivances that protect against potential for failure that is an inevitable accompaniment of increasing complexity. To be sure, part of that growing complexity may be invested in safety assurance—in building malfunction controls into the system operations and proliferating backups and redundancies. But problems are inevitable in this domain as well. The prospect of things going wrong will always "slip through the cracks," and complex systems for this very reason grow increasingly error prone and susceptible to malfunction.

The results of this situation are not difficult to discern. Increasingly complex systems pose ever greater prospects of mishap. We devise those more complex systems because we need them. But their very existence poses new problems. We soon come to depend on them, and this dependence renders us increasingly vulnerable to frustration. Complex systems are inherently less amenable to successful comprehension, management, and control. It is evident that where double the number of steps must go right in a goal-pursuing context, we double the prospects of something going wrong, other things be-ing equal. Complexity generally enlarges the prospect of system failure—and where not in frequency, there in magnitude of effect. A washing machine can malfunction far more readily than a washboard—and with more extensive consequences. There is no clearer indication of the vulnerability that com-plexity engenders than the extent to which a single act of sabotage by a ter-rorist, or of dishonesty by a greedy or disgruntled employee, can inflict de-structive damage on a large enterprise or an extensive organization.

Evolutionary biologists have insisted that organisms achieve their devel-opment at a price—that as the process of natural selection and adaptation ties a creature ever more firmly to the conditions of its environmental niche there comes an ever-increasing complexity. More "highly developed" creatures thus pay for this status by becoming more complex, and this in turn creates a line of adaptability that renders them increasingly vulnerable. More primitive species—say viruses in comparison with humans—are vastly more adaptable and thereby far less at risk under environmental change. And this principle that complexity makes for vulnerability is clearly not confined to the biolog-ical domain.

Risk is a natural companion to complexity. It involves the (multiplicatively interactive) combination of two factors: the probability of failure and the magnitude of the consequences should failure occur. Increasing complexity generally enlarges risk. It does so not necessarily by increasing the probabil-ity of failure but by increasing the negative consequences should failure oc-cur. (Precisely when the probability of failure is diminished we tend to in-crease our stake on success.) Increasing complexity thus tends to be associated with increasing risk.[4]

Our individual activity—say getting from home to work—is undoubtedly simplified by the technology of the automobile in contrast with that of the horse. But the entire system of automotive transport is something vastly more complex, penetrating pervasively into every aspect of our social and eco-nomic lives. Local simplicity rides on the back of globally systemic com-plexity. The present day motor vehicle code of U.S. states is more complex than the whole of their transport legislation in the 1890s. And no American who lived through the months of the Arab oil embargo can fail to realize the magnitude and power of the vulnerabilities to which such systemic complex-ification renders us subject.

This state of things engenders inevitable threats and dangers. Specifically, with the ongoing sophistication of human artifice we find that:

- With *cognitive* systems we face the threat of disintegration, disorganization, and cognitive dissonance.

- With *technical* systems we face the threat of breakdown and malfunction.
- With *social* systems we face the threat of gridlock and stalemate or—at the opposite extreme—of chaos and anarchy.

Throughout the domain of human creativity—alike in matters of cognitive, technological, and social engineering—we encounter an increasing complexity that carries with it the inherent risks of system malfunction.

The basic point that is at issue here is relatively straightforward. It is that in general and as a rule complex systems are by reason of their very complexity more expensive and more difficult to construct, operate, and maintain. And they are also more risky to use—not necessarily by way of an increased likelihood of malfunction but rather through the increased seriousness of the consequences that ensue when a malfunction occurs. In sum, the increased complexity of our systems does not come cost free; to achieve its undoubted advantages we have to pay a substantial price, not in terms of money alone, but also in terms of risk.

## 4. CONCRETIZATION QUANDARIES AND DECISION GRIDLOCK

At the earlier, less sophisticated stages of technological progress, it was easier for people to understand the implications of change. When changes occur in highly complex systems there is bound to be an obscurity of consequences. It becomes somewhere between difficult and impossible to say in advance just what the result of modifications and innovations will be. We all too frequently cannot see our way clearly through the accompanying ramifications to grasp the implications of innovation for their management. Effective decision making requires the timely processing of full information. And both of these factors—acquiring and processing information—tend to be more difficult and cumbersome in contexts of complexity. And the more complex the ramifications of a choice situation are, the more likely it is that any particular way of resolving it will be worrisome to some of the individuals or groups who have a stake in its outcome. Few of us have the engineering sophistication to be rocket scientists. But effectively none of us today has the technical sophistication to be a social engineer. And there is a real possibility that even all of us taken collectively do not have what it takes.

In particular, the measures that are required to cope with matters of social and economic policy become increasingly complicated and constantly more expensive to implement and difficult to operate. The complexities that have to be taken account of outrun the grasp of ordinary understanding. (Think, for example, of Hillary Clinton's health care program, not to speak of the federal tax code.) The management of U.S. systems in the area of medical or social or economic processes and programs has grown so difficult throughout the successive decades that the political system is nowadays close to throwing up its hands in frustration.

And so the very power of technical progress leads it to carry new disabilities and incapacities in its wake. The operational dynamics of complexity expansion mean that as we increase our problem-resolving capacity we will inevitably—preferences to the contrary notwithstanding—also increasingly lose our grip on the overall effectiveness of problem control. In fact, none of us can form an accurate picture of how proposed changes of process and procedure in the management of complexity will work themselves out—both for the society at large and for themselves and those in whom they take an interest. And even where we ourselves think that we can see the way clear, there will be precious few others who agree with us.

This state of affairs manifests itself in a striking and by now familiar phenomenon that might be called the *cacophony of experts*. The difficulties of rational problem solution in complex situations engenders a variety of plausible but competing alternative possibilities. And in the absence of a single clear-cut resolution a dissonance of theories arises. Pundits come upon the scene with their competing wares—each with a case that seems plausible and persuasive but is nevertheless insufficiently clear-cut and decisive to drive its opponents from the field. The destabilizing effect of technological change thus paves the way to social discord and procedural impotence. Here sheer stagnation is the natural result of risk-aversive "better the devil we know" thinking. All too often, life in our imperfect world proceeds in such a way that to all appearances certain abstractly desirable aims simply cannot be concretely realized by acceptable means. Let us inspect the ramifications of this process a bit more closely.

As noted above, technological progress increasingly complicates the processes of social choice and decision. In an environment of increasing technological complexity we must develop ever more sophisticated control processes to address new problems. Such changes affect different people, different groups, different constituencies differently. And just here the eventual effects of the measures we take to address the challenges become lost in a fog of unpredictability. For every winner there are some losers and various others who—not being able to see the way clear—come to feel threatened. When people confront more complex problems they find it difficult and sometimes impossible to think their way through to satisfactory solutions. Everyone feels put to risk by some aspect of the ill-understood consequence flow of potential innovation. And in the face of this perplexity, people become fearful lest any step away from the status quo—unhappy though the existing state of things may be—will plunge them into disaster.

This sort of situation is an open invitation to gridlock.

What might be called a *concretization quandary* arises when it is—abstractly considered—a good idea to do $A$ and the only way to do so concretely is by doing $A_1$ or $A_2$ or $A_3$ (etc.), while nevertheless doing each of these alternative $A_i$ is a bad idea. In such situations there is no concrete way of realizing a generically desirable objective. A certain act that is generically positive can nevertheless be accomplished only in various particular ways each of which is something that is—individually—negative.

Think here of the story of the princess whose father is a kingly ogre who will release her from his paternal thralldom only on the condition of her marrying the princeling of some neighboring kingdom. But it turns out that all of the available princelings are quite ineligible: one is too ugly, another too stupid, a third too loutish, and the like. For the princess, marriage is seemingly a good idea. Yet each of the actually available alternatives for achieving this otherwise desirable objective is unsuitable and unacceptable. Or again, consider the plight of the younger son of an impoverished aristocrat. He finds himself so situated that taking up an appropriate career is somewhere between eminently desirable and absolutely necessary. But each of the specifically available alternatives is infeasible: he is too cowardly for the army, too hydrophobic for the navy, too skeptical for the church, and so on.

The schematic structure of such concretization quandary situations is clear. The circumstance that now arises is that while realizing $A$ is desirable in the abstract, it nevertheless remains false that any and every *particular A* realization is in itself something desirable. Those who face such a quandary situation are emplaced in the unhappy position where a certain end, absolutely viewed, looks good—but only as long as one ignores the problematic details of its concrete actualization. There is simply no acceptable way to get there from here.

Such concretization quandaries reflect the *logical* impracticability of adopting pervasively the (seemingly) natural principle of (seemingly) democratic process: *Majorities represent the will of the group; if the majority wants it done, then so be it—let it be done.* In various cases the majority indeed wants $A$ done, and this can be achieved only by allowing $A$ in one or the other of its particular forms $A_1, A_2, A_3$ and the majority is against doing each and every one of the $A_i$.

It is easy to see how such concretization quandaries affect the workings of democracy in the context of the voting process. Situations frequently arise when policy-making reaches a stage where even though a social program or public work is generally acknowledged as something that is abstractly (or generically) desirable and desired, yet nevertheless each and every one of the concrete ways of realizing it is deemed unacceptable. Downsizing the market in illegal drugs, keeping teenage girls out of maternity wards, or reducing the exploding public expenditures for medical services are only a few examples of this. Here on the question of achieving a result $R=$ somehow versus maintaining not-$R$, a decided majority is in favor of $R$. But equally, each and every one of the concrete ways of realizing $R$ is opposed by a comparable majority. This sort of situation is something often encountered in the political arena, where we frequently read in the press stories such as:

When asked what Congress should do about the federal deficit, two-thirds of the voters preferred cuts in major spending programs, but this support for spending cuts dissipated whenever it came to specific programs, with two-thirds of the voters opposed to each of the specific ways of achieving these cuts.

Despite an accepted "Sense of the Congress" resolution, no implementing decision can manage to gain congressional approval. In such a situation, society confronts a concretization quandary: there simply is no majoritatively acceptable way of reaching a majoritatively accepted goal.

The problem, of course, lies in the fact that in practical affairs abstract desiderata have to be realized in concrete circumstances. And in such concrete circumstances we never have that abstract desideratum in and by itself; rather its concretization is invariably accompanied by a penumbra of circumstantial detail—we never have *just A* but always $A$-with-$Z$ for some circumstantial addendum. And the prospect arises that each and every *available* alternative involves a circumstantial addendum that offsets and negates the positivity at issue with $A$ viewed in the abstract. The realization of what is, in and of itself, a perfectly proper desideratum $A$ may—in the existing circumstances—saddle us with collateral negativities, with the result that there just is no acceptable concretization of this desideratum. With a concretization quandary the best course may well be to leave well enough alone.

A larger lesson emerges. Our life proceeds in an imperfect world where certain abstractly desirable acts cannot be concretely realized because each and every one of the available specific and concrete ways in which this realization can actually be achieved involves collaterally incidental deficits that negate—in those particular circumstances—the general benefit at issue. From the practical point of view, the world's arrangements may prove to be far from ideal.

Desiderata are mere wishes—mere indefinite wants: "Would that $A$ were realized." But means require concreteness: some certain *particular* for that abstract desideratum to be concretely realized. And the abstract may be acceptable by and even desirable to us while nevertheless we shrink from any one of the concrete states that would bring this abstraction to realization in the actually prevailing circumstances. It is evident that in adopting an end we do not endorse any and every possible means for its realization. (Think here of W. W. Jacobs's classic short story "The Monkey's Paw.") And sometimes the circumstances can be so radically unfavorable that despite our espousing a certain desideratum as such we cannot find even a single acceptable means for its realization. A drastic economy of scarcity obtains with respect to end-realizing concretizations.

But does the problematic nature of the concrete version not mean that we have abandoned those ends as abstract desiderata? Not at all! It means no more than that in the circumstances we defer those ends—put them into abeyance and hope for the coming of a more favorable context. But it does not mean that we abandon those ends in the abstract. We suspend their operation but do not abrogate them as ends.

## 5. A RETROSPECTIVE REFLECTION

The present deliberations have revolved around four significantly problematic issues:

1. Complexity escalation
2. Obscurity of consequences and cognitive chaos
3. Concretization quandaries
4. Decision gridlock and immobilization

This condition of affairs obviously has substantial and significant implications for the general polity of social decision. In particular, it brings to the fore the question of how a sensible society can proceed in the face of technological progress that impels us into a sphere where the problem field that confronts us may come to outrun the power of our cognitive capacities for problem resolution.

And this situation seems to obtain on the basis of general principles. The instruments we forge for the solution of our problems—intellectual and physical—all prove effective only up to a point. And as new problems arise they will require new resources, new methods and devices. But in the natural evolution of things, the creation of ever new and more powerful instruments becomes increasingly difficult. And there is every reason to think that eventually—in the long run of things—the hurdle will be raised to a height that we simply cannot leap. Our standard resource of problem solving—the use of process-modeling intelligence—may come to prove unavailing. A point may—and potentially will—be reached where the familiar role of modeling and calculation will no longer prove adequate as a problem-resolving instrumentality.

In the twentieth century, the Austrian school of economists argued that the domain of economic phenomena is inherently of so intricate and sophisticated a nature that such theorizing as it is practicable for us to manage really cannot provide an adequate grasp on the phenomena—and certainly not one powerful enough to guide our interventions in establishing effective control. Human phenomena are inherently so complex, volatile, and variegated that the project of capturing them within the confining boundaries of universal laws is unrealizable. The complexity of the system of social processes at work in the operations of an advanced modern economy is such that there simply is no way for us to calculate the behavior of the system. No model that we devise will be adequate to handling the requisite details. As they saw it, the very idea of a social science of human behavior is a pipe dream.[5]

We return here to the "bounded rationality" that arises in decision situations when the complexity of a problem situation substantially exceeds the reasoning powers of the problem solver. And here, often as not, the best strategy is to let "matters run their course" and use the observation of its processes as a guide for the formation of our policies and programs. Where calculation based on theory is impracticable, the best we can usually do is to observe broad tendencies and let the course of experience be our guide.

A strong case thus obtains for saying that this sort of situation holds not just in economics but far more broadly throughout the social domain. Here too there are, fortunately, other ways of solving problems than by "figuring it out" through human artifice and calculation. One of these is to leave the solution of the problem to "the course of events" (either in nature or in a simulation model of some sort) and then simply sit back and watch what happens. Where the calculations become too complicated for us, such a recourse to the practice of "watchful waiting," of examining how the matters work themselves out when left to their own devices, is a variant and sometimes highly useful cognitive resource. In situations of near-impenetrable complexity, our practice in matters of public policy will generally be guided far more effectively by localized experimental trial and observation than by the theorizing resources of intellectual technology.

## 6. PRAGMATIC ANOMALIES

Pragmatic anomalies can arise because it is wise on occasion to do something that seems foolish. They can result from the fact that even appropriate rules can admit appropriate exceptions in practice. There is, clearly, no conflict or contradiction on grounds of the general principles between the theses:

1. It is wise (advisable, prudent, appropriate, advantageous) *in general* to follow the rule *R*.

2. It is wise (advisable, prudent, appropriate, advantageous) *on occasion* to
   violate the rule *R*.

In general, even the best rules of practice will be subject to exceptions. But
it is also true that exceptions require rules: there can be no exception where
there is no rule and no excuse where there is no norm. It is in *this* sense
that the classic dictum that the exception *proves* the rule must be construed. Exceptions have to be exceptions *to* something; it lies in the nature
of things that they can arise only in the context of established norms.

On this perspective, it emerges that it is one thing to endorse the appropriateness of a directive as a general rule of practice, and something rather different to establish that the rule must be obeyed in every case and, in particular, in the case that is now before us. Generality is one thing and universality
another where rules of action are concerned.

Our present concern will, however, be with something very different from violating a rule with a view to ulterior purposes. Consider the athlete who throws
the game to win a bet or avert a threatened blackmail. Or again, consider the
driver who exceeds the speed limit to rush an injured person to hospital. In such
cases we have the situation of a general rule ("Play to win," "Drive legally")
being set aside with a view to an overriding purpose introduced *ab extra* from
outside the range of operation for which the rule was instituted (game competition or everyday driving). Here we make exception to the rule because some
weightier purpose (financial gain or protecting life) intrudes upon the scene to
overpower the aims and objectives that motivate the rule in question. This sort
of thing will not concern us here. Rather, the focus of the present deliberations
is with situations where there just is no rule-overriding domain-*exterior* purpose
outside the rule's own purposive orbit. Accordingly, the issue that primarily
concerns us is that of domain-*interior* rule-overriding considerations. Consider
some examples of this phenomenon:

- The military technician who departs from a practice that sensible strategy
  would dictate to "throw his opponent off balance"
- The gambler who breaks the rules of good play to keep from being predictable to the opposition in the interests of more effective gaming
- The artist or actor who breaks the rules "for effect"—to keep from being
  boring and to escape from routine, i.e., to make the performance more
  entertaining

Once we admit the cogency of such situations, we confront a significant context-specific limitation as regards the compellingness of otherwise appropriate rules.

What we have here is a breakdown of the principle of pragmatic universalization, which stipulates: (*R*) Always do in each particular instance that which would be appropriate (would work out for the best) as a general practice—one that is duly stipulated in an appropriate rule.

As the preceding counterexamples indicate, this metarule is *not* a universally valid principle. It lays down a sensible rule—but one that itself admits of exceptions.

Given that it does not hold in general, just when—that is, for what generic *class* of rules—does the metarule *R* hold good? In what sorts of circumstances are exceptions admissible? And this confronts us with the further question: Are there any rules of praxis that hold with exception-precluding force?

Perhaps exceptionlessness arises with rules of a very high level of generality, such as "Do the prudentially appropriate thing." After all, one might think that if that "exception" were justifiable, then it would, ipso facto, come to represent the prudentially appropriate thing. But this is not so. Think again of the military tactician who fails to do the prudentially right thing to throw the opponent off balance. The point is that "the prudentially right thing" may itself become a problematic conception when a "higher prudence" has us cast *ordinary prudence* to the winds.

But what of something as generic and all-encompassing as "Do the morally right thing." Surely morality, unlike prudence, is sacrosanct. Surely a moral rule cannot be overriden! Or can it? To be sure, a whole series of moral theorists stretching from the Immanuel Kant of the *Grundlagen* to the Kurt Baier of *The Moral Point of View* sees the dictates of morality as all-predominant and inherently nonoverridable. But is this indeed so?

We come here to a large and difficult issue: Can a vast *prudential* advantage override a small *moral* transgression. (Could I defensibly break my promise to meet you at a certain place and time when keeping it would—in the unforeseen and perhaps unforeseeable circumstances—cost me a fortune?) Or can a great but nevertheless supererogatory benevolence override a small moral transgression. (Could I defensibly act—quite above and beyond the call of any duty—to ensure a great [but otherwise unmerited] benefit for many at the cost of violating a trivially small commitment to someone?) Kant gave an emphatically negative answer. For him morality is categorically sacred with no transgressions—however small—admissible for any extenuous reasons. Moral rules (properly formulated) admit no exceptions. That makes moral acts universalizable, and indeed this universality—this principle that what is proper in a given case is proper always and exceptionlessly—is for Kant a key test of morality. But this position is deeply problematic. It runs against our moral intuitions that morality is a matter of *fiat justitia ruat caelum*. It seems deeply problematic to insist that one must do the morally right thing though the heavens fall.

But the issue can be made to assume a somewhat different aspect. Consider what is ordinarily thought of as a moral rule—for example, "Do not inflict pain!" But what of doctors and dentists who do inflict pain, but only in the patients' best interests. Kant had a cagey strategy for circumventing this difficulty—that of building the *motive* into the characterization of the action at issue. "Do not harm others just for your own pleasure." "Do not inflict pointless pain on others." Insofar as motivation is pivotal for morality this seems to make for categorical rules. Kant's idea was that properly formulated moral rules—or "maxims" as he called them—will themselves involve specifying the motive/reason for the action and thereby preclude exceptions, seeing that there will now be no prospect of a "conflict of rules" or of "overriding considerations." This Kantian strategy is to all appearances an effective and serviceable strategy for arriving at nonoverridable rules.

But of course what makes these Kantian rules or maxims of morality exceptionless is that it lies in the nature of the case that the exception must look not just to action but also to motivation. (It is not "Do not kill" that is the rule but "Do not murder," and not "Do not hurt people" but "Do not hurt people simply for your own pleasure.") And this is, in a way, cheating. The resultant rules will be not just rules of action (behavior) but rather rules of motivation proceeding with reference to what is to go on imperceptibly in an agent's mind, confined to the internal form of thought's thought.

Yet, what if we insist on looking for rules of *overt action* in the public forum— rules governing the sort of agent comportment that can be observed and perceived by others? At this point we would concentrate our focus upon matters of overt behavior and observable praxis, putting aside all matters of unobservable plans, purposes, and intentions by focusing upon what people actually and overtly *do*. Are there any exception-precluding ("unbreakable") rules here?

One plausible place to look in the effort to get at such unbreakable rules is in a very different domain of praxis, namely, games. Take chess rules for example. "Always move bishops diagonally." Such a rule is exception precluding simply because any *seeming* violation takes us outside the realm of reality (viz. chess playing) for which the rule is apposite. This clearly is an "unbreakable" and thus exception-precluding rule. Of course it is not *physically* impossible to move the bishop otherwise, but it is impossible within the framework of the game. If one were to violate this rule one would, ipso facto, no longer be playing chess. Here we come to the important difference between game-defining rules and rules of strategy, seeing that breaking the rule means not playing at all rather than merely not playing well.

And we find yet another context that is substantially similar to this games-playing situation in the case of mathematics. Consider the rules: "Do not divide by zero," or "Do not come up with 5 when multiplying 2 by 2." Such rules too are unexceptionable—not in that incompetents cannot make mistakes, but rather in that in breaking such rules one has thereby ceased playing the arithmetic game.

The point is that, with any project whose very nature is defined (as per chess or arithmetic) by rules that provide for definitionally rigid constituting specifications, it will be impossible, in the very nature of things, at one and the same time to violate the rules and to continue functioning within the enterprise at issue. With any such conventional practice, the rules in effect constitute that practice as the thing it is. But prudence and morality are not like that. They are enterprises that root not in *conventions* but in the requirements of human life (achieving our purposes, interacting appropriately with our fellows, etc.).

The difference between a nature-mandated and an artificial mode of praxis is thus crucial for the purposes of the present considerations. The rules of an artificial (artifactual, man-made) activity such as games playing (chess) or symbol mongering (speaking German) or mathematical manipulation (arithmetic) can afford to be practice definitive — and thereby peremptory and unexceptionable — because if you violate the rules then you are out of the practice and you can chose to do this. Artificial practices, unlike natural ones (breathing, eating), are *optional*: you can chose simply not to engage in them. But those nature-mandated ones are not. Accordingly, the former (optional) practices can manage to have unexceptionable rules of the violate-the-rules-and-you-are-out-of-the practice type. But the letter (mandatory) practices cannot manage this, seeing that the practice is inescapable, as it were: one just can't extract oneself from it. The rules of games, in short, can afford to be practice defining and exception precluding, but the rules of life (and thus of prudence and morality and cogent reasoning) cannot afford to do so.

Here, then, we have the key that unlocks our problem. The exceptionless rules are those that define an essentially arbitrary and thus strictly *conventional* (and thereby optional) practice of some sort. But the world's complexities being what they are, any inherently natural and thereby inescapable rules of action will admit of exceptions — will have to be rules of thumb.

## 7. THE FACTS OF LIFE

Life is holistic. Its teleological structure of needs and wants is complex, many-sidedly systemic; its components and aspects are symbiotically interrelated. It has no place for unbending rigidities. It is not conventional but natural. And so its departments are not autonomous (separable, hermetically sealed) and compartmentizable but rather symbiotically interconnected. They are organically interactive. What goes on at one place can be affected — and eventually offset — by what goes on elsewhere. The rules of here may have to give way to the demands of there.

The rules of practice in life—of prudence, morality, etiquette, etc.—do not fall into hermetically sealed compartments. They are not rules of an artificial, conventional praxis that is purposively self-maintained. And so, in the praxis of life and its major departments—prudence and morality included— pragmatic anomalies can always arise. In the praxis of life, all rules have their exceptions—though, of course, this circumstance neither destroys the validity of those rules as rules nor abrogates the need to respect them for what they are. The problematic character of Kant's ethics lies in its commitment to those strong idealization principles that we examined at the outset. A viable practical doctrine designed for operation in the real world cannot appropriately hitch its wagon to the star of idealization to that extent.

The overall lesson can be put simply:

• Those situations and circumstances of human life that set the stage for practical deliberations are so diversified and complex that "external" considerations can always come upon the scene.
• Hence exceptions can always arise.
• Hence pragmatic anomalies can always arise.

In life—unlike games—the rules are made to be broken. But never, of course frivolously—since otherwise those rules would not be what they are. Exceptions will generally arise. But they will only do so appropriately when they are rooted in cogent and sufficient reasons. To *this* rule there are no exceptions.

## NOTES

1. For a good survey of the issues see Klaus Mainzer, *Thinking in Complexity: The Complex Dynamics of Matter, Mind, and Mankind* (Berlin, etc.: Springer Verlag, 1994).

2. On complexity in relation to social and political issues see H. R. Kohl, *The Age of Complexity* (New York: New American Library, 1965).

3. Think here of Parkinson's Law as discussed in C. Northcote Parkinson, *Parkinson's Law* (Boston: Houghton Mifflin, 1957).

4. For a variety of vivid illustrations see Charles Perrow, *Normal Accidents Living with High-Risk Technologies* (New York: Basic Books, 1984).

5. See K. R. Popper, *Conjectures and Refutations: The Growth of Scientific Knowledge* (New York: Harper Torchbooks, 1965); F. A. Hayek, "The Theory of Complex Phenomena," in *Studies in Philosophy, Politics and Economics* (London: Routledge & Kegan Paul, 1967), pp. 22–420; F. A. Hayek, *The Counter-Revolution of Science: Studies on the Abuse of Reasons*, 2d ed. (Indianapolis, Ind.: The Free Press, 1979). On these issues see Alexander Rosenberg, *Philosophy of the Sound Sciences* (New York: Westview Press, 1988; 2d ed. 1995).

*Chapter Nine*

# Is Consensus Required for a Rational Social Order?

## 1. THE QUESTION OF PRACTICAL CONSENSUS

The idea has been astir in some European intellectual circles for many years that a just and democratic society can be achieved only on the basis of a shared social commitment to the pursuit of communal consensus. Such a view insists that the public harmony required for the smooth functioning of a benign social order must be rooted in an agreement on fundamentals. Progress toward a congenial and enlightened society accordingly requires an unfolding course of evolving consensus about the public agenda—a substantial agreement regarding the practical question of what is to be done.

This general line of thought traces back to Hegel, who envisioned an inexorable tendency toward a condition of things where all thinking people will share a common acceptance of the manifold of truths revealed by Reason. Sailing in Hegel's wake, the tradition of German social thought reaching through Marx to the Frankfurt School and beyond has reinforced the idea that the realization of a communally benign social order requires a commitment to consensus—a shared public commitment to the idea that the pursuit of consensus in communal affairs is a great and good thing.

This position, however, is deeply problematic. It is mostly so for theoretical reasons. One obviously has to worry about what it is that people are consensing about and why it is they are doing so. (Think of the precedent of Nazi Germany.) But there are also tremendous practical obstacles. In the matters that really and truly divide people into deeply disagreeing groups—abortion, gun control, the death penalty, and the like—we are simply not going to reach consensus. The respective sides take irreconcilable positions that, for them, are simply nonnegotiable. The yearning for consensus in such matters reflects pie-in-the-sky unrealism. And so it is fortunate that a good case can be made for the contrary view that a benign social order need not be committed to the quest for consensus, but can be constituted along very different, irreducibly *pluralistic* lines. After all, the idea that a consensus on fundamentals is realistically available is in fact false with respect to most large, complex, advanced societies and is (so we shall argue) simply not needed for the benign and "democratic" management of communal affairs. And even the idea that consensus is a desirable ideal is very questionable.

To be sure, the widely favored allocation of a pride of place to consensus sounds benevolent, irenic, and socially delectable. Indeed, it may sound so plausible at first hearing that it is difficult to see how a person of reasonableness and goodwill could fail to go along. Nevertheless, there is room for real doubt as to whether this utopian-sounding position makes sense. Serious questions can be raised as to whether the best interests of a healthy community are served by a commitment to consensus. Consensus, after all, is no be-all and end-all in and of itself. Truth—and correctness in general—is not *constituted* by agreement, but at best *evidentiated* by it because we expect reasonable people to be concerned for what is true or otherwise appropriate.

To begin at the end, let it be foreshadowed that the policy whose appropriateness will be defended here is one of a *restricted dissonance* based on an acceptance of a diversity and dissensus of opinion—a benevolent (or at any rate resigned) acceptance of the disagreement of others with a credo of respect to beliefs and values. Such an approach envisions a posture of diversity conjoined with "live and let live," taking the line that a healthy democratic social order can not only tolerate, but even—within limits—welcome dissensus (disagreement, discord), provided that the conflicts involved are kept within "reasonable bounds." This discussion accordingly maintains the merits of the consensus-dispensing view that a benign social order can be unabashedly pluralistic and based not on the pursuit of agreement but on arrangements that provide for an *acquiescence in disagreement*. This position sees as perfectly acceptable a situation that is not one of judgmental homogeneity and uniformity, but one of a dissonance and diversity that are restrained to a point well short of outright conflict and chaos.

## 2. PRODUCTIVE VERSUS UNPRODUCTIVE MODES OF CONFLICT

Dissensus has to be said for it, at least, that it is at odds with a stifling orthodoxy. A dissent-accommodating society is ipso facto pluralistic, with all the advantages that accrue in situations where no one school of thought is able to push the others aside. Indeed, the extent to which a society exhibits tolerance—is willing and able to manage with aconsensual diversity arising from free thought and expression—could be seen as a plausible standard of merit, since a spirit of mutual acceptance and accommodation is one of the hallmarks of a benign and productive social order.

It must be acknowledged, of course, that dissensus does have a negative side. Its negativities preeminently include:

- the danger of escalation from productive competition to destructive conflict
- the possible diversion of resources (effort and energy) into potentially unproductive forms of rivalry
- the separatist fragmentation of the community into groups estranged from each other in a posture of mutual hostility
- the tendency to dismiss otherwise meritorious plans, projects, and ideas simply because they originate from the "outside," from a rival, competing source

Clearly, the story is not altogether one-sided. However, the sensible way of handling the question of consensus versus dissensus calls for effecting an appropriate balance between the positive and the negative aspects of the issue, seeking the productive advantages of tolerating dissent while averting its potential negativities by ad hoc mechanisms fitted to the specific circumstances at hand.

This said, the fact remains that it is highly problematic to maintain that a rational public policy must be predicated on a striving for consensus. Situations where the public good is best served by a general acquiescence in disagreement are not only perfectly possible but also often actual. Life being what it is, it would be too hard on all of us to be in a position where we had to reach agreement in matters of opinion and evaluation. A society in which the various schools of thought and opinion try to win the others over by rational suasion is certainly superior to one in which they seek to do so by force or intimidation. But this does not automatically make it superior to one where these groups let one another alone to flourish or founder in their divergent individuality. After all, the striving toward consensus produces a sometimes debilitating uniformity of thought, and the tolerance of diversity permits the flourishing of an often fruitful variety of individual plans, projects, and visions. Pluralism also can often better serve the currently prevailing interest of individuals, securing for them and for their society the potential future benefits accruing from a stimulating competition and productive rivalry.

## 3. ACQUIESCENCE AND CONTROLLED CONFLICT

Consensus by its very nature is a condition of intellectual uniformity, a homogeneity of thought and opinion. And just herein lie some of its significant

shortcomings. The fact is that the impulsion to consensus will in various circumstances prove itself to be:

- an impediment to creativity and innovation. (Settling into a consensus position is a discouragement from endeavoring to outdo others and striving to
  improve on their efforts by "doing one's utmost to excel.")
- an invitation to mediocrity. (By its very nature, realization of consensus involves a compromise among potentially divergent tendencies and thus
  tends to occupy "the middle ground" where people are most easily brought
  together, but where, for that very reason, the element of creative, insightful
  innovation is likely to be missing.)
- a disincentive to productive effort. (One of the most powerful motives for
  improving the level of one's performance is, after all, to come under the
  pressure of competition and the threat of being outdone by a rival.)

Nor is the idea of a consensual polity-originating "social contract" of
much help. As a historical event it is a bizarre fiction. And as an idealized
standard its merit resides wholly in the normative question of what reasonable people *should* agree on, which is something that has to be settled independent of consensuality as such. In politics as elsewhere the basic issue is
what people should agree on owing to its inherent merits—on what merits
agreement. The contingencies of actual agreement do not provide for what is
needed here.

Not only is insistence on the pursuit of general consensus in practical matters and public affairs unrealistic, but it is also counterproductive. It deprives
us of the productive stimulus of competition and the incentive of rivalry. In
many situations of human life, people are induced to make their best effort
in inquiry or creative activity through rivalry rather than emulation, through
differentiation rather than conformity, through a concern to impede the folly
they see all around. Productivity, creativity, and the striving for excellence
are—often as not—the offspring of diversity and conflict.

Most human intellectual, cultural, and social progress has begun with an
assault by dissident spirits against a comfortably established consensus.
The Andalusian friar Bartolomeo de las Casas upheld the human rights of
Amerindians against the consensus of Spanish conquistadores and settlers
alike that they were inferior beings; the eighteenth-century American abo-
litionists protested the institution of slavery in the teeth of a vast prepon-
derance of powerful opponents; J. S. Mill's protest against the subjection
of women was a lone voice crying out in a wilderness of vociferous males.
And lest it be said that such "eccentric" but benevolent views did all eventually win through to a general consensus of thought and universality of

practice, one can instance the teachings of Jesus, whose endorsement is largely a matter of words and not deeds. We can have no comfortable assurance about the present—or future—consensual victory of truth, justice, and the cause of rightness.

When we find ourselves dissenting from others, we may dislike their opinions and disapprove of their actions—and they ours—but we can, by and large, manage to come to terms. We can—often, at least—"get along" with others quite adequately when we can agree to disagree with them or when we can simply ignore, dismiss, and sideline our disagreements—postponing further opposition to another day. What matters for social harmony is not that we agree with one another, but that each of us acquiesces in what the other is doing, that we live and let live, so that we avoid letting our differences become a *casus belli* between us. *Acquiescence* is the key. And this is not a matter of *approbation*, but rather one of a mutual restraint that, even when disapproving and disagreeing, is willing (no doubt reluctantly) to let things be, because the alternative—actual conflict or warfare—will lead to a situation that is still worse. All is well as long as we can manage to keep our differences beneath the threshold of outright conflict.

The crucial fact about acquiescence is that it is generally rooted not in agreement with others but rather in a preparedness to get on without it. What makes good practical and theoretical sense is the step of (on occasion) accepting something without agreeing with it—of going along despite disagreement—an acquiescence of diversity grounded in a resigned toleration of the discordant views of others. The merit of such tolerance is not (as with John Stuart Mill) that it is an interim requisite for progress toward an ultimate collective realization of the truth, but simply and less ambitiously that it is a requisite for the peace and quiet that we all require for the effective pursuit of our own varied visions and projects.

A deep strain of utopianism runs through social contract theory, be it of the Rawlsian form favored among North American social philosophers or the Habermasian form that has been so infuential on the European continent. Historical experience, empirical understanding of the human realities, and theoretical analysis of our social situation all conjoin to indicate that an insistence on agreement among rational inquirers and problem-solving agents is simply futile. However inconvenient this may be for the philosophers, ample experience indicates that we shall never actually achieve a firmly secured general consensus—and not only in matters of politics, art, and religion, but also in a whole host of cognitive domains such as history, economics, social science, and philosophy itself. And there is no reason to think that a benign society can exist only where the clash of private opinions and preferences is eliminated or suppressed by the processes of social coordination. A healthy social order can perfectly well be based not on agreement but on the sort of mutual restraint in which subgroups simply go their own ways in the face of dissensus.

Neither in intellectual nor in social contexts, after all, have we any firm assurance that a consensual position somehow represents the objectively correct or operationally optimal solution. To be sure, in many cases some sort of resolution must be arrived at with respect to public issues. But we need not *agree* about it: a perfectly viable result may be had simply on the basis of a reluctant acceptance of diversity. What matters for the smooth functioning of a social order is not that the individuals or groups that represent conflicting positions should think alike, but simply that they acquiesce in certain shared ways of conducting the society's affairs.

## 4. SOME OBJECTIONS

We come, at this juncture, to what is a central point in the rational defense of the present position. It pivots on the following objection put forward by a hypothetical critic:

I agree with much of what you have said on the merits of dissensus and diversity. But you have failed to reckon with the crucial distinction between a consensus on matters of ground-level *substance* and a consensus on matters of *procedure*. As you maintain, a benign social order can indeed dispense with a substantive consensus regarding *what* is decided upon. But what it indispensably requires is a procedural agreement on modes of conflict resolution—a second-order consensus about *how* those first-order issues are to be decided. If the society is to serve effectively the interests of those involved, and if mutual strife and conflict are to be averted, there must be a consensus on *process*, or the validity of the procedural ways in which these base-level resolutions are arrived at. Consensus on particular decisions may be dispensable, but consensus on the decision-making *process* is essential.

Despite its surface plausibility, even this more sophisticated argument for the necessity of an at least procedural consensuality is deeply problematic.

For one thing, even where there is a consensus about process, there may nevertheless be sharp disagreement regarding matters of implementation. Even where people agree on, say, maintenance of law and order, civility of interaction, an equitable distribution of resources—and many other such "procedural" principles of human action in the public domain—such procedural agreements are much too abstract to define particular public policies. (We can agree on the need for "law and order" and yet [quite plausibly] disagree sharply on questions of civil disobedience and the limits of appropriate protest.) Process consensus is a lot to ask for—but still is not sufficient for a benign social order.

But the problem goes deeper yet. Process consensus is not necessary either. It is simply false that procedural agreement is indispensable for a benign social order. To manage its affairs in a mutually acceptable way, a community needs no agreement on the merits of those procedures as long as there is acquiescence in their operation. What matters is *not* that we agree on methods— I may have my favorite and you yours. I might, for example, think that the proper way to address the issue at hand is for the electorate to decide it by referendum; you think that the right and proper way is by a vote in the legislature. But as long as we both acquiesce in the established process of having the courts decide, all is well. There is no *agreement* here: we emphatically do not concur in thinking that the courts are the proper (let alone the best!) avenue for a solution—in fact, *neither* of us thinks so. What we do is simply acquiesce to letting the courts make their decisions on the issue. What matters for irenic conflict resolution is not second-order consensus but second-order acquiescence. A sensible defense of acquiescence is accordingly not predicated on ignoring the distinction between first-order substantive issues and second-order methodological ones; rather it is prepared to turn this distinction to its own purposes and to see it as advantageous rather than inimical to establishing the claims of acquiescence vis-à-vis consensus.

But even when we agree to disagree do we not in fact agree? Not really. Or, rather, we do so in name only! An agreement to disagree is as much an agreement as a paper dragon is a dragon—the whole point is that there is no agreement at all here. Parties who agree to disagree do not *agree* on anything—they simply exhibit a similarity of behavior in that they walk away from a disagreement.

Another possible objection to an emphasis on acquiescence as a mechanism of social decision runs as follows: To cast acquiescence in a leading role in the management of public affairs is to invite the deployment of raw power; to open the doors to coercion, oppression, domination, and the subjection of the weak to control by the strong. But this view of the matter is simply unjust. The rational person's acquiescence is, after all, based on a cost-benefit calculation that weighs the costs of opposition against the costs of going along. And to deploy raw power is to raise the stakes—to readjust not only the benefits but also the costs of acquiescence. As those who study revolutions soon learn, it is precisely at the point when power is made blatantly overt—when bayonets are mounted and blood shed in the streets—that acquiescence is most gravely endangered. It is clear that discernibly just, benign, and generally advantageous arrangements will secure the acquiescence of people far more readily and more extensively than those that infringe upon such obvious social desiderata. It is quite false that an approach that roots social legitimacy in acquiescence somehow favors oppression and injustice.

To be sure, much will depend on the sorts of people with whom one is dealing. If they are unreasonably long-suffering and spineless—if they are weak-kneed and cave in easily under pressure—then a social order based on acquiescence is one in which they indeed can be oppressed and exploited. (But then, of course, if they are totally accommodating and yielding, a consensual order based on agreement with others is also one in which their true interests are likely to suffer.) The fact remains that sensible people are distinctly unlikely to acquiesce in arrangements that are oppressive to them. An acquiescence-oriented political process does not provide a rationale for domination, exploitation, and oppression precisely because these are factors in which sensible people are unlikely to acquiesce—once brought into play they soon call forth opposition rather than accommodation. One of the early lessons that an acquiescence-based society learns is that its ethics are not smoothly viable if people are constantly testing the limits of acquiescence. An emphasis on being civilized, urbane, and restrained is not at odds with acquiescence but is actually conducive to the enterprise.

Moreover, the complaint that a polity of acquiescence inherently favors the perpetration of injustices cannot be sustained. Acquiescence is like agreement in this, that nobody else can do it for you. People may be able to rearrange the conditions under which you will have to proceed in this regard, but how you proceed within those conditions is always in the final analysis up to you. As recent developments in Eastern Europe all too clearly show, people will acquiesce in injustice only to a certain point. After that they turn to noncooperation and opposition—they take up arms against the sea of troubles or perhaps simply emigrate. The limits of acquiescence are finite.

Admittedly, acquiescence can be bad—it can be forced or compelled. It is no automatic route to political legitimacy. But then of course neither is consensus. We are always entitled to ask why people agree: is it for good and valid reason—a concern for truth or for fairness, say—or is it because of self-interest, conformism, constraint, or propagandism. Legitimacy is always an additional issue; and just as it is not just consensus one wants but a consensus that is rational and free, so it is not just acquiescence one wants but acquiescence that is given in a way that is sensible and uncoerced.

## 5. A POLITICAL PERSPECTIVE

A great continental divide runs across the landscape of the philosophical tradition. On the one side lies the Platonic tradition that looks to systemic order through a rational coordination under the aegis of universal principles. On the other the Aristotelian tradition looks to organic balance and an equilibration of diversity and division. The one is geared to a classicism of holistic order, the other to a pluralism of countervailing checks and balances. The one favors the rational uniformity of a harmonious consensus, the other the creative diversity of a limited dissensus. The one invokes the tidiness of theorizing reason, the other the diversified complexity of actual history.

Given this divide, European political thought since the time of the Enlightenment has been fixated upon the idea of the "general consent" of the people in defining a general agreement of the community (*la volonté générale*), which may or may not be all that apparent to the people themselves (and may need to be discerned on their behalf by some particularly insightful élite). All the same, the danger of that idea, run amok, is apparent to anyone who has looked even casually into the history of the French Revolution.

The polity of consensus proceeds from a fundamentally socialistic commitment to the coordination and alignment of individual action with the uniform social order of "rationalized" central planning (albeit, no doubt, a uniformization that is not imposed, but rather engendered—presumably— through the "hidden hand" of an idealized rationality). Legislatures, taxing authorities, and political theorists all like to keep the affairs of the citizenry neat and tidy. But the fact of the matter is that the impetus to public consensus, agreement, and concurrence of thought will not be high on the priority list of the true friends of personal freedom and liberty. And so, the polity of pluralism abandons the goal of a monolithically unified "rational order" for the "creative diversity" of a situation of variegated rivalry and competition. Its political paradigm is not that of a command economy with its ideal of rationalization and uniformizing coordination, but that of a free market with its competitive rivalry of conflicting interests. Consensuality looks to uniformity of thought, pluralism to reciprocally fruitful harmonization of discordant elements.

Rather different sorts of policy approaches are at work in social orders based on consensus-oriented and acquiescence-oriented principles. Consensus-seeking societies will aim to maximize the number of people who approve of what is being done; acquiescence-seeking societies seek to minimize the number of people who disapprove *very* strongly of what is being done. The one seeks actual agreement; the other seeks to avoid disagreement so keen as to preclude acquiescence. The two processes sound similar but are in actual fact quite different in spirit and in mode of operation.

Consensual polity seeks to induce people into agreement. A polity of acquiescence sees this as unrealistic and accordingly takes a different line. It takes the object of sensible polity to call for creating circumstances in which the price of acquiescence in disagreement looks feasible to all concerned in comparison to the available alternatives, so that rational people will be led not to agreement but to willing—if reluctant—acceptance.

The social requisite of a viable public order can on this basis plausibly be viewed as lying not in the fostering of consensus, but in the forging of conditions in which people become willing and able to acquiesce in dissensus through recognizing this as a state of affairs that is not only tolerable but even in some way beneficial. Consensus simply is not a requisite for the prime social desideratum of having people lead lives that are at once personally satisfying and socially constructive.

The notion that consensus is a valid ideal—that the endeavor to bring about a uniformity of thought and opinion is an unqualifiedly good thing—is deeply problematic. Consensus is not in general a goal whose pursuit should regulate the way in which we actually proceed in the conduct of our cognitive and practical affairs. In many contexts the interests of the entire community are best served by a fragmentation of beliefs and values within its ranks. For example, the social welfare of a group is usually most effectively catered to when different political subunits can, though pursuing different policies and adopting different programs, provide testing grounds for the evaluation of alternatives. And the communal welfare of a group is generally more effectively served when different religious or cultural sects or schools of thought can provide congenial homes for individuals with different personal needs and inclinations. Consensus can be the cause of boredom, inaction, stagnation, and complacency. It can result in a narrowing of horizons and a diminution of options that are destructively stultifying—that substitute bland uniformity for an invigorating variety.

The situation differs in this regard as between theoretical and practical philosophy. A resort to idealization in theoretical philosophy—in matters of inquiry, truth, and rationality—is something of a harmless bit of theoretical ornamentation. But in matters of practical philosophy idealization can do actual harm. No doubt, an ideal can be a useful motive in the direction of positive action, but generally only as a *primum mobile*—an initiator. To hold to the hard and fast, in season and out—not just at the start of the process of decision and action but all along the line—can be dangerous and self-defeating. By diverting our attention away from the attainable realities, a preoccupation with the unrealizable ideal can do real damage in this domain, where a pursuit of the unrealizable best can all too easily get in the way of the realization of attainable betterments and impede the achievement of realizable positive objectives. It might be nice for me to be a good polo player, but if this lies beyond my means and talents, it would be foolish to let this desideratum get in the way of my perfectly feasible and attainable goal of being a good tennis player. It would be a splendid thing to be a great artist, but for many individuals it would be counterproductive to let this aspiration get in the way of being good craftsmen. Similarly, it might be nice to have social consensus, but it would be counterproductive to let this get in the way of social amelioration—of effecting various smaller, but perfectly feasible, improvements in the arrangements of a pluralistically diversified society.

Insofar as consensus is something positive, then, it has to be seen in the light of a wishful-thinking desideratum rather than a valid aspiration of the sort at issue with an ideal. The polity of consensus is too utopian to provide me with so useful an instrument.

On this perspective, one arrives at a less tidy, less optimistic, but nevertheless truer and more realistic picture of our social condition, one that accepts without regret the dissensus of a restrained rivalry among discordant and incompatible positions, none of which is able to prevail over the rest. The upshot is one of reciprocal acquiescence in a pluralistic community of conflicting views—a situation in which each party is content to accept a diversity that affords them the benefit of pursuing their own projects at the cost of according a like privilege to others.

## 6. THE POLITICAL DIMENSION

The consensus-downgrading position articulated here opposes a utopianism that looks to a uniquely perfect social order that would prevail under ideal conditions. Instead, it looks to incremental improvements within the framework of arrangements that none of us will deem perfect but that all of us can live with. Such an approach exchanges the yearning for an unattainable consensus for the institution of pragmatic arrangements in which the community will acquiesce—not through agreeing on its optimality, but through a shared recognition among the dissonant parties that the available options are even worse.

With "other things equal" or "in ideal conditions," agreement is certainly better than disagreement and consensually achieved resolutions preferable to those obtained in less agreeable ways. But theorists who maintain this sort of position—subject as it is to saving qualifications—seldom admit how precious little follows from it. Other things are seldom if ever equal and conditions seldom if ever ideal. In this imperfect world, we live and labor among complex sub-ideal circumstances. And so, what matters first and foremost is not the design of utopia but the devising of mechanisms for coping with the problems of the real world. And in dealing with these actual problems a recourse to idealizations can be both unprofitable and counterproductive. What is wanted here is not utopianism but the design of institutions that can induce real-world, imperfect, crassly motivated individuals into courses of action that serve the general benefit. And at *this* level, a recourse to programs and policies based on acquiescence has much to be said for it.

No doubt, the millenarians among us would yearn for a society organized on the principle of having people do what ideally rational agents would do in idealized conditions. But most of us recognize that this is simply pie in the sky. The pragmatic theory is clearly more realistic than its idealized rivals, seeing that it requires no recourse to perfectly rational agents and ideal circumstances. It is willing and able to function in the real world, pivoting its operation on a factor (the minimization of serious dissatisfaction and discontent) that is readily understood and relatively simple to assess.

The key consideration for the conduct of interpersonal affairs is that the activities of people can harmonize without their ideals about ends and means being in agreement. It is a highly important and positive aspect of social life that people can and do cooperate with one another from the most diverse of motives; agreement need not enter into it at all. What is needed for cooperation is not consensus but something quite different—a *convergence of interests*. And it is a fortunate fact of communal life that people's interests can coincide without any significant degree of agreement between them (a circumstance illustrated in both domestic and international politics by the frequency with which allies fall out once the war is over).

The sensible posture, then, is to be realistic in the face of pluralism and dissensus—to accept the unavailability of agreement and to work at creating a communal framework of thought and action where we can come to terms with discord and make the best—and most—of it. Such a position calls for a profound change of methodological attitude to a distinctively different sort of social-engineering objective. The guiding principle is no longer "Let us do whatever we can to promote consensus," but rather "Let us do whatever we can to render dissensus harmless—and even, wherever possible—profitable." It is simply—and mercifully—wrong that consensus is the requisite for a stable society and a healthy body politic. It is simply—and mercifully—wrong that pluralism is the manifestation of an inherently harmful social malfunction.

To be healthy and productive for the body politic at large, a modern plurinatural and pluricultural society has to achieve peaceful coexistence and amicable collaboration among people who differ not just in opinion but also in interests, in life-style, in ideology, in religion, in culture, etc. To predicate their political situation on the achievement of consensus is to postpone it to a day that will never come. To be sure, people are not moved by intent alone; ideologic and larger values also matter. But people are not stupid. And in circumstances where they realize that the price that must be paid for the opportunity to cultivate ones values and to transmit them to one's posterity is to accord the same privilege to others—where the choice is between pluralism and disaster—they are likely to prefer the lesser evil.

The aim of practical politics is not, and cannot realistically be, to bring people into a condition of consensus, of actual agreement on the issues. Instead, the prime political imperative of our time is to create conditions of social life in which people who disagree with one another on issues small and large can nevertheless achieve conditions of beneficial consistence, and be able to live with one another not just in peace but even in ways that prove mutually beneficial. The watchword should not be harmonious *consensus* but productive *coexistence*.

*Chapter Ten*

# Risking Democracy
# (Some Reflections on Contemporary
# Problems of Political Decision)

## 1. SETTING THE STAGE

It is worthwhile to consider the consequences that follow from two theses—two premises, as it were—that represent facts with far-reaching implications for the way in which we Americans nowadays conduct our political business. These two premises are as follows:

1. Some of the political mechanisms on which we traditionally rely in matters of public policy decision can no longer function as effectively as they once did because under present conditions their operation often as not results in gridlock.
2. The decision problems that we face in contemporary public affairs are often too complex to allow a resolution by way of rational calculation and what might be called the application of "scientific principles."

Both of these theses offer pretty bad news. And both are somewhat controversial. Nevertheless, I am convinced that a good case can be made for each of them. Let me begin with the first.

## 2. THE PERVASIVE THREAT OF GRIDLOCK

The actual mode of operation of our political system—at every level from city hall to national legislature—is such that all too often a small but determined minority can effectively block a measure. By exploiting alliances based on horse-trading methods to gain allies for their cause, special interest groups can effectively impede the adoption of measures to which they object. And in American experience, at least, this phenomenon has become increasingly prominent over the years.

Consider, for example, something so simple as a road. Everyone may be agreed that a highway is needed to connect point $X$ and point $Y$. Technical study shows that there are three ways to achieve this, but nobody wants that road in his backyard. So three interest groups immediately form to keep the road out of their respective proximities. If they are anything like equally strong, each will be worried about the other two ganging up on them. The only safe step is to band together to scotch the project as a whole.

This is bad news, but there is even worse. Let us forget about blockage by small groups and turn to a strictly *majoritarian* decision process.

For the sake of an example, consider the situation of table 10.1.

That $A$ be realized in some way or other is (so we here suppose) favored by the group, i.e., by the majority of those involved (viz. $X_1 - X_3$, that is, three out of five). Thus, on the question $A$-somehow versus not-$A$, a decided majority is in favor of $A$. But, equally, each and every one of the concrete ways of realizing $A$ is opposed by a majority (likewise three out of five). In such a situation our minisociety finds itself in what might be called a *concretization quandary*: there is no majoritatively acceptable way of reaching a majoritatively accepted goal. Gridlock situations of this sort often pose a condition in which, despite an acknowledged *abstract* desirability, there is no concrete implementation found acceptable. And experience shows that this sort of gridlock that blocks the realization of a generally desired result is in fact all too often encountered in the political arena.

Such concretization quandaries reflect the *logical* impracticability of adopting pervasively the (seemingly) natural principle of (seemingly) democratic process: *Majorities represent the will of the group; if the majority wants it done, then so be it—let it be done.* As the previous examples show, it can readily happen that a majority indeed wants $A$ done, yet this can be achieved

**Table 10.1.  A Hypothetical Situation in a Mini-Electorate**

| Alternative Realization Modes | | People's Acceptability Assessments | | | | |
|---|---|---|---|---|---|---|
| | | $X_1$ | $X_2$ | $X_3$ | $X_4$ | $X_5$ |
| $A$ | $A_1$ | − | + | + | − | − |
| | $A_2$ | + | − | + | − | − |
| | $A_3$ | + | + | − | − | − |

Note that most people favor the majority of $A$-modes.

| | $X_1$ | $X_2$ | $X_3$ | $X_4$ | $X_5$ |
|---|---|---|---|---|---|
| $A$-somehow | + | + | + | − | − |
| not-$A$ | − | − | − | + | + |

only through one or another of its concrete realizations $A_i$ and a majority is against doing each and every one of the $A_i$.

Recent American experience affords numerous instances—health care, Social Security safeguarding, and education reform among them—where there is on the one hand a virtually overwhelming public pressure, duly recognized by Congress, that something be done to resolve a certain problem, while nevertheless each of the available solutions is deemed unacceptable since in each case some combination of groups manages to defeat each one of the concretizations of that generally agreed desideratum. Every *available* solution generates an opposition sufficiently powerful to defeat it. The upshot here defeats the plausible principle that "to will the end is to will the means" because each and every one of the particular means to that accepted end is itself deemed unacceptable. At this stage of our history the realities confront us with fragmented society where gridlock is the order of the day because powerful interest groups are able to frustrate motion in any given direction.

It is tempting at this point to envision the following sort of objection: "But surely those issues here depicted as intractable are far from being so. There is nothing inherently unmanageable about such issues as gun control, health care, illegal immigration, etc. Plenty of countries have devised perfectly sensible polices."

Quite so—this may very well be the case. Such problems may not be intractable in themselves and by nature. But that is beside the point. The point, rather, it that such problems are—or have become—intractable not by nature but in context—that is, they are intractable for a society that has a particular sort of composition and a particular sort of political modus operandi. After all, what is intractable in selling $X$ need not be so in selling $Y$.


### 3. COMPLEXITY AND ITS CONSEQUENCES

When this republic was launched and the first Congress convened in New York City in March 1779, there were 20 senators and 59 representatives. Today we have 100 senators and 435 representatives, an increase of clearly substantial proportions. And in this case, at least, the advertising slogan for the movie *Godzilla* applies: *size matters*. The bigger the group the more likely is its splintering into constituent blocks and the less likely the chances of configuring a larger subgroup of like-minded individuals willing and able to impose a definite resolution on controversial issues.

And this brings me to my second thesis.

In view of the sort of gridlock situation that we have been considering, one constantly sees our political system being hamstrung in it efforts at problem solving. And as a result of this, the legislative branch has tended increasingly to withdraw from decision making and to hand over the problems to the courts.

But how do the courts actually go about deciding public issues when the political system washes its hands of them? They, in turn, incline to pass the buck to acknowledged authorities. They rely on experts to provide the guidance that is, in the circumstance, both necessary and desirable. Increasingly, however, this recourse to experts itself proves unavailing. Not that there aren't any—or that those there are are unwilling to offer solutions. In general there are lots of them and they all have a good deal to say. The problem is rather one of surfeit. The unfortunate fact of it is that the experts almost invariably disagree. They offer us conflicting judgments and discordant solutions that cancel each other out. And this occurs not because the experts are incompetent but because the problems are intractable. They are of such complexity that scientific analysis and expert deliberations simply cannot settle matters.

The trouble with complexity is the difficulty it creates for decision making by rational calculation. Consider the example of the young person who confronts the choice between two job offers or between two marriage partners. Here a vast number of pro and con considerations can come into play. There are simply too many operative factors and too many convoluted interrelationships for the issue to be resolved by rational calculation: there is, all too often, no rationally determinable resolution to such a choice problem. The nature of relevant details and the elaborate feedback relationships involved in the intricacy of their interrelationships prevent rational calculation from affording a viable means of resolution.

Take something as "simple" as demographic prediction. On its eightieth anniversary in 1931 the *New York Times* asked various specialists to envision the world after another eighty years, in 2011. Their sociographic expert predicted a U.S. population of 160 million for that year. In fact, it reached 260 million in 1994 and by 2011 might well reach 320 million—double that estimate.[1] In the mid-1990s America's economic gurus saw annual budget deficits stretching as far as the eye could see, but by the end of the decade we were in surplus. In the middle of the century demographers envisioned a population explosion of Malthusian proportions; but by the end of the century the world's population was stabilizing and many advanced countries were facing the prospect of population deficits.

The root reason for the long-term unpredictability of significant social developments is not hard to uncover. For one thing, chance and chaos come into it: the course of events over the longer term in matters of social interest depends too much on subtle interactions that, while virtually indiscernible at present and negligible in the short term, can make an enormous difference to what happens over the long term. But something deeper is also at work. Brute contingency is the main culprit. Genuinely self-developing systems contribute formatively to their own development over time. Their futures are not preordained by their pasts because novelty–spontaneity–creativity intervenes. Such systems—whether biological, technological, or social—inevitably have aspects that are unpredictable because there are always some situations to which they make ad hoc responses and about which they simply don't make up their minds until they get there, as it were. Complexity is the inseparable accompaniment of modernity. We encounter it throughout our science, throughout our technology, and throughout our social and cultural environment as well. Perhaps the clearest manifestation of this is the range of choice that nowadays confronts us on all sides in everyday life—with sources of information, means of entertainment and leisure activities, occupations, and even life-styles. Modern life has become vastly more complicated with the widening of range of choice and opportunity.

People incline to think that technological progress makes life easier. It is faster and more convenient to cross oceans by plane than by sailing ship, to phone messages rather than mail letters, to type with word processors than write with quills. But while all his is true enough, there is the other side of the coin as well. In some cases, enhanced performance is acquired at the cost of elongated training. Technological progress constantly destabilizes the status quo and brings changed processes, procedures, and products in its wake. Individual actions are generally simplified at the cost of complicating larger processes. Not only does the gain in efficiency that technical progress engenders provide us with more time to do things, but it also vastly increases the range of things that can be done and the power of the means for their realization. The fact is that progress itself pushes us deeper and deeper into difficulties. Every solution opens up new problems.

New-gained technical capacity accordingly brings additional problems of management. Notoriously, one virtually has to be a rocket scientist to program one's VCR. A modern car has many thousand parts, but a jet aircraft can have over four million and a space rocket over six million. Only technical experts can carry out repairs or modifications and in this regard the era of string and sealing wax is over. Moreover, what holds for function holds for malfunction as well. In the pre-jet era when an airplane plummeted from the sky, a pair of experts had comparatively little trouble figuring out what went wrong. But as the explosion of TWA Flight 800 demonstrated in 1996, determining the cause of the malfunction of a system as complex as a modern high-tech aircraft can take a team of scores months or even years. In combat, the pilot of a fighter jet makes more decisions in five minutes than a sailing-era ship's captain did in a day.[2] And so, while technological progress—be it material or social—may indeed simplify and facilitate the performance of particular tasks, its aggregate effect is to make large-scale processes more complicated and difficult.

In his amusingly written but brilliantly perceptive book, C. N. Parkinson took note of what might be called the managerial bloat of modern organizations.[3] In all sorts of enterprises as management has flourished activity has diminished. Throughout the twentieth century, the British navy had ever more admirals as ever fewer ships were in commission. As operations downsized, management upsized.

We can see the impact of complexity all about us. The computerized control electronics in a contemporary automobile cost some two thousand dollars more than the steel used to produce the same car. Today, it is not boondoggling or diminished capacity that produces managerial bloat but the inexorable demands of dealing with greater complexity. And sometimes the functional complexities of a system make its effective control virtually unrealizable.

Granted, computer-automated problem solving is one of the wonders of the age. Computers fly planes, land rocket modules on the moon, win chess competitions, develop mathematical proofs. All the same, we have to come face to face here with what might be called a *Hydra effect*, after the mythological monster who managed to grow several heads to take the place of each one that was cut off. The fact is that there is a feedback symbiosis between problems and solutions that operates in such a way that the growth of the former systematically outpaces that of the latter. Accordingly, those sophisticated information and control technologies not so much resolve problems of complexity as enlarge this domain by engendering complexity problems of their own. Despite the enormous advantages that they furnish to intellectual efforts at complexity management, computers nevertheless do not and cannot eliminate but only displace and magnify the difficulties that we encounter throughout this sphere.

The long and short of it, then, is that, in the presence of the intractable problems presented to us by the highly complex social system of the modern world, our technical resources are of limited utility and even experts are not of all that much help when it is solutions we are after. Their expertise—powerful though it may be—is unable to calculate answers when there are none to be found.

Examples of intractable issues that figure on the agenda of present-day public concern are easy to come by. They include such matters as:

- how best to address the drug problem,
- what steps to take toward alleviating inner-city poverty,
- how to "save" Social Security as the ratio of young-to-old becomes increasingly adverse,
- how best to combine the interests of job protection and environmental safety,
- how to bring illegal immigration under control,
- how to reduce the danger of handguns.

Often as not we find that in such matters of public policy decision even the most well-intentioned measures result in unforeseen and unfavorable consequences. Social medicine like chemical medicine frequently comes with unhappy side effects. So-called reforms all too often go wrong. We "liberate" mental patients from institutionalization and turn them into street people—or worse. We institute child support for the most disadvantaged and destroy the family structure that exists in this sector of society. We endeavor to control immigration and "rationalize" entry into the country and thereby create greater hordes of illegal immigrants.

How often have we experienced the scenario of adopting expert-recommended answers to social problems only to see them go disastrously wrong? The fact is that in a complex modern society there is often no way to get a rational grip on the consequences of public policy measures and employ "scientific intelligence" to foretell consequences. There are no calculable solutions here—all we ever seem to get is a clash of my experts versus your experts. Rational calculation and scientific analysis leave us in the lurch. The best we can do is to feel our way cautiously step by step— to experiment, to try plausible measures on a small scale and see what happens, and to let experience be our guide.

## 4. REVIEW

A brief retrospect is in order. It yields a picture that has two main components:

1. Our political system is functioning under conditions that render it prone to gridlock. We all too often confront a condition of affairs where powerful minority interest groups are able—singly or in combination—to prevent the legislative process from moving in any one particular direction.
2. The inherent complexity of issues of public policy decision is such that we cannot count on experts to arrive at convincing resolutions to public policy

questions. The complex patterns of contemporary policy decision are simply too complicated for resolution by the sort of rational calculation that one can reasonably hope to obtain from experts. Too many factors are involved in volatile interaction in too complex interrelationships.

Just where—mere perplexity apart—does this condition of things leave us? Clearly in something of a quandary. When problem solving with respect to public issues is necessary, while nevertheless the legislative system is unwilling and its expert-guided judicial supplement unable to provide a solution, the situation is clearly an unhappy one. Can anything be done that is more constructive and hopeful than wringing our hands in bafflement and gnashing our teeth in frustration? Is there any practicable way of energizing a gridlock-prone system into action?

When one sees how Congress ties itself into knots over issues such as campaign finance reform or medical insurance rationalizations or when one sees how state legislatures hamstring themselves over issues such as electoral reappointment or gun registration, one finds oneself exclaiming, "There has got to be a better way." And there assuredly is. But to realize it we have to take a step back and take a hard look at the first principles that characterize democrative institutions at their most fundamental level.

## 5. THE LESSON

Ever since the infancy of political theory in the era of Plato's *Republic*, political philosophers and theoreticians have manifested a deep aversion to genuine democracy. Dismissing the generality of people as "the masses" (hoi polloi—the great unwashed), they have insisted on the need to have matters decided by wiser heads (invariably, it seems, those belonging to people very much like themselves). No matter how loudly they enthuse about "the people," "the citizenry," and "the common man," political gurus have insisted, almost without exception, that in matters of actual decision it is necessary to have others act on their behalf.

The great irony of the history of political thought is that democrats do not trust democracy—or at least do not trust it in the real world as it is actually constituted. Even the most liberal of democrats shrink back when it comes to accepting real flesh-and-blood democracy. Marxists want "power to the people" alright, but want themselves to exercise it on their behalf. Liberals want democracy—but only in a *representative* form where liberals carry the burden of representation. Idealistic philosophers such as John Rawls want the fundamentals of public policy decided democratically alright—but by hypothetically idealized elections operating in hypothetically idealized circumstances. The pragmatist John Dewey was less unrealistic. But even he took the line that if electoral democracy is to function properly then "we"—the intelligent, scientifically informed élite—must "educate the masses" to the point where people hold the views that an educated élite deems appropriate.

Now, as I see it, what is called for on the basis of a realistic reaction to the prevailing state of affairs is a thoroughgoing revision of this point of view. A viable defense of democracy must be prepared to take people as it actually finds them. The great political need—and opportunity—of our time is, I submit, the possibility of accepting a realistic rather than an idealized version of democracy.

Democracy has always had a difficult time of it. It does not accord something with our standard political categories based on the left–right spectrum. Leftists have generally looked to élites and mistrusted the fundamental conservation of the silent majority. Rightists have never been prepared to entrust traditional fundamentals to a potentially excitable populace. But difficult times call for difficult measures. The old maxim holds: the best way to make people trustworthy is to trust them. Conditions may well be ripe for actually trusting the people, and to bring to realization the idea of "power to the people"—an idea that has always been anathema to the left of politics and its right alike.

What these considerations argue for is revolutionary in its implications, but it is not actually a revolution. It is a mere strengthening of those mechanisms—*initiative* and *referendum* with respect to legislation and *recall* with respect to legislators—through which the will of the people can achieve a more powerful and direct expression. In particular, it would greatly facilitate the problem-solving process by making it possible—and comparatively easy—for issues to be put on the ballot and decided by vote. All of these processes exist to some extent in the present scheme of things, and I am suggesting no more than that their operation be extended and strengthened whenever possible.

To say this sort of thing is nowise to oppose exploiting the guidance of expert opinion. By all means, let the experts study, propose, explain, argue. Far be it from any academic to gainsay the utility of experts and deny the necessity of making use of their worthy labors. We very much need them to indicate alternatives, clarify issues, assess consequences, evaluate assets and liabilities, and generally work to inform the public debate on the issues. But we emphatically do *not* need them to decide matters. By all means let them do their work and have their say about it. But when this is said and done, then by all means let the people decide. Populism, I submit, is an idea whose time has come.

I am under no illusion that such a step is an easy one. The idea of popular democracy gives politicians fits. In the oversimplified orthography of our political caste (and note that it is becoming a caste system, with more and more second- and third-generation politicians in high public offices) "populism" is a four-letter word. The idea of actual popular democracy is decidedly unwelcome to the political establishment. While "public opinion" interests its members deeply (why else all this money and effort spent on polling), it interests them principally as a means toward heading off any direct public involvement in the more active stages of the political process.

And in this context it should be noted that giving the general citizenry a greater role in legislation increases the probability that there will be motion on some issues on which the political establishment prefers immobilization. These include such matters as election reform with special emphasis on spending limitations and term limits; tax reform with special emphasis on compliance simplification and tax reduction; and very likely also some real measure of medical insurance reform. It is likely, therefore, that one's reaction to the proposed measures of legislative populism will be formed less through considerations of the general principles of political theory than by one's views regarding such concrete issues.

There is, of course, always the danger that some "hot button" issue may excite public opinion and lead to problematic decisions. The traditional theory is that the intermediation of elected representatives provides for cooler heads that make sensible decisions. But this theory itself begs some large questions because the sagacious and disinterested representatives that it assumes are not all that readily available. Moreover, an important point deserves emphasis. What is being proposed here does *not* affect the separation of powers that is the cornerstone of our system. It leaves the executive and the judiciary wholly unaffected, and only intrudes upon the legislative process, the very part of our system whose operation is most direly in need of reformation in the present condition of public affairs.

One significant asset of a more populist mode of legislation has to do with the simple matter of numbers. The gridlocks and stalemates that so often arise root largely in the role of special interests. And to identify the source of difficulty here a simple prescription suffices: Follow the money. Clearly, it is easier to bribe, pressure, or otherwise influence a legislature of a couple of hundred people than an electorate of many millions (particularly where those comparatively few are perpetually cash hungry thanks to the costs of campaigning). Of course money can also be expended to influence the public at large, but it is going to take a lot more of it.

In the early days of our republic no great disadvantage attached to stalemates. Inaction led to preservation of the status quo, and in a traditional agrarian society there is nothing so bad about that. But in a complex and dynamic modern world where matters all too often are going from bad to worse, stability is not a particularly pleasant option, and inaction can prove to be disastrous.

The reality of it is that in the existing condition of affairs, an important advantage belongs to any system that produces actual decisions. When society does not settle its problems satisfactorily people naturally incline to blame government. The result is a deep distrust and even antagonism to our "public servants." Gridlock and inaction in the face of pressing problems readily result in disgruntlement and disaffection. But unfairly so. It is not the case that our public functionaries are generally corrupt or incompetent. There is no proper room for a conspiratorial paranoia that holds that our political representatives are in the pockets of some powerful conspiracy. The fault lies *in the system* and the conditions in which it has to function rather than in the persons who operate it. It is the system that needs to be fixed, and a greater infusion of democracy is our best prospect for fixing it.

Undoubtedly, a more democratic mode of procedure will also lead to mistakes. But the choice we face is not between some mistakes and none; it is between an inaction that is often the most dangerous proceeding of all and a policy that offers a chance to avert immobilization. The reality of it is that in these matters of political decision there are no foolproof arrangements. It goes almost without saying that the present proposals will not bring utopia to realization. But be this as it may, matters stand on a very different footing when the public makes decisions directly. When things go wrong—when even our best-conceived measures do not deliver on their promises and live up to expectation—then in a system of genuinely participatory decision making "we the people" will at least have no one to blame but ourselves.

In summary, the position of these deliberations is as follows:

1. In the prevailing condition of things there is no reason to think that a more democratic mode of proceeding in matters of public policy decision will do any worse than the existing modus operandi.
2. There is good reason to think that greater democracy will help to overcome what is a grave defect of the present process—namely, its tendency to get bogged down in the inertia of stalemate and gridlock.
3. From the standpoint of what is abstractly desirable—namely, an enhancement of a genuinely democratic process that gives people a substantial voice in the management of their affairs—the more overtly participatory arrangements being proposed have much to be said on their behalf.

And on this basis, it seems plausible to suppose that the present situation is decidedly propitious for what is simply yet another Jacksonian reformation of our political system, a further substantial extension of popular democracy.

To be sure, there is a great deal more to democracy than figures in the present context—it is, after all, a matter of ethics and ideology and not just a style of process for decision making in the public policy domain. But it certainly does have that dimension as well. Acceptable processes of public choice in general and of voting in particular are not the be-all and end-all of democracy. But nevertheless, one cannot have a democracy without them.

## NOTES

This chapter was given as a Distinguished Lecture in Public Affairs at the State University of New York at Albany on April 23, 1999, and subsequently published in the *Public Affairs Quarterly* 12 (1999): pp. 297–308. Reprinted by kind permission of the publisher.

1. See Josh Rosenthal, "Looking Forward, Looking Back: *The New York Times Magazine* 1896-1996-2096," *The New York Times Magazine*, September, 29, 1996, pp. 45–46 (see p. 45).

2. On complexity in relation to social and political issues see H. R. Kohl, *The Age of Complexity* (New York: New American Library, 1965), as well as the author's *Complexity* (New Brunswick: Transaction Publishers, 1998).

3. C. Northcote Parkinson, *Parkinson's Law* (Boston: Houghton Mifflin, 1957).

*Chapter 11*

# Collective Responsibility

## 1. THE ISSUE

Is the U.S. military at large to blame for the massacre at Mi Lai? Do Americans in general deserve reproach for the plight of the country's Indian reservations? Whom can one fault for the decline of civility in America's cities or the slippage of mathematical competence in its high schools? It is problems of this sort that are at issue in the present deliberations, whose focal questions are as follows: What is involved in a group's being responsible—ethically responsible—for producing a collective result? What conditions must be satisfied for it to be appropriate for us to praise or blame a group for some result of its doings?

In addressing this problem, the natural step is to begin by basing our understanding of group responsibility upon that of individual responsibility. Here, at the level of individuals, responsibility for a result is clearly a matter of *producing the result through one's own deliberate agency*—barring the intrusion of defeating aberrations such as, for example, duress or deceit. For responsibility to enter in, it is not enough that that untoward result be *produced*, as the causal result of an individual's actions; it must also be *intended* in some appropriate fashion. Carrying this idea over to groups, one thus needs to address two pivotal issues: group agency and group intention. Unfortunately, neither is anything like as simple and straightforward as one might wish.

## 2. PROBLEMS OF GROUP AGENCY

The "responsibility" at the center of the present discussion is of the sort that opens the door to evaluative and normative appraisals, so that praise and blame will be pivotal considerations.[1] The merely causal "responsibility" of productive contribution is of course neutral in this regard—a merely necessary but not sufficient condition. For authentic responsibility some element of intentionality must always attend to causal participation—the factor of *productive intentionality* is crucial.

All the same, causal or productive involvement is an important part of the picture. And as regards causality, the first thing to note is that a group can bring it about that a certain result obtains without any member of that group having any significant or substantial contributory relationship to the production of that result as such. Thus, if every dweller in a town adores his neighbor's cats and hates his dogs, they can collectively produce the result that all the town's cats are loved and all its dogs hated—even though this may occur in such a way that no one ever desires—or even contemplates—this result. And the same sort of thing happens if every driver happens to be out on the road and a traffic jam results. Moreover, in such a case no one contributes more than a minute share to the result, and sometimes, interestingly, the smaller the individual shares—the more people on the road, say—the worse the result. Such situations are legion; groups regularly manage to produce results with which, *as such*, their members have little or nothing to do.

The fact is that when a group collectively produces a certain result, none of its individual agents need do anything that bears significantly on that result. Indeed, often this result is something the individuals could not facilitate if they wanted to—which they well may not. Consider "The affidavits made by Tom and Jerry created a conflict of testimony." Clearly neither agent—acting on his own—did anything that was in and of itself conflict engendering. Again, suppose that a hardware store carries ten hammers and that ten customers come along and buy them. Among them they have exhausted the store's supply of hammers. But of course nothing of this sort figures in any of *their* thoughts or actions. In all such cases it makes no visible difference *as far as the individual agent is concerned* whether that contributory act obtains in isolation or in an unwitting, merely fortuitous concert with other agents in producing an untoward aggregate result. The inherent status of contributing individuals' doings is clearly not affected one way or the other by the essentially accidental circumstances of context. And even should it eventuate that the collectivity is a disaster, the fact remains that the individual's own act may well be perfectly innocuous—in particular when that infinite result was totally unforeseeable. Neither in production nor in contemplation need a group's individual members play a significant role in such cases.

The circumstance that an individual's act constitutes a contributing part of a certain overall result represents a feature of that act alright—but a *contextual* feature of it. And this context is in general something over which the individual in question has no control or even significantly productive influence. (Think, for example, of the "wave" created by spectators at a sporting event, where each individual simply stands up and raises his or her arms—or, even more drastically, think of what happens when a foreign expression enters a language as a "loan word.") Moreover, the contributory aspect of the action may well lie entirely outside the individual's awareness. (That individual's contribution to the wave may simply be an aping of his neighbor in mere social conformity.)

## 3. PROBLEMS OF GROUP INTENTIONS

Suppose that someone comes across a nearly unconscious sufferer on a country lane. After providing an effective but rather slow-acting medical remedy, he goes off to get further assistance. Then another person comes along and does exactly the same. But these remedy doses, though individually helpful and appropriate, create a jointly fatal overdose. The two people acting together have, in effect, caused the sufferer's demise by their well-intentioned actions. And this is the polar opposite to what they intended or expected. This "Good Samaritan Mishap" illustrates the sort of thing that can—and often does—happen with interactively produced results, where product and intention can readily diverge.

For intention and responsibility, then, distributive activities that collectively engender a result by way of causal production are clearly not enough. Overt purposiveness in relation to this result must be added. Suppose that $X$ wants $p$, $Y$ wants $q$, and that they act accordingly. Joined together the group $X$-and-$Y$ wants $p$-and-$q$. Yet neither $X$ nor $Y$ may want this outcome or anything like it. (Indeed, wanting it may be senseless, as when $q$ happens to be not-$p$.) Accordingly, the overall upshot may well be something seen by both as eminently undesirable, as when $X$ wants to kill $Y$, and $Y$ to kill $X$. With groups of agents, the separate intentions of individuals cannot simply be combined. Here, wholes have features that, as far as intentionality is concerned, are nowise mere sums of the parts.

Group responsibility clearly calls for coordination and depends on the extent to which the group acts as a unit within which the actions of individuals are concerted. With the product of a merely fortuitous confluence of individual actions (e.g., a bank run), group responsibility is clearly out of the picture. The element of collaborative coordination—of a "conspiracy," so to speak, in producing the result—is called for. The difference between acting as a coordinated group and acting only as a collection of disjoint and disaggregated individuals is crucial here.

With group responsibility as with individual responsibility, this factor of intention is critical. The weaker the element of intentionality, the weaker that of responsibility. Thus consider the series

- Active and deliberate participation in the production of a result
- Passive agreement in its production
- Detached spectatorship
- Reluctant acquiescence (going along)

Responsibility clearly fades as we move down the line here. The closer the "degree of association" of the individual with the production of a collective result, the greater the responsibility (and the greater the extent of blame or credit).

From the causal point of view, individual contributions appear to sum up productively. The individual agents make their causal contributions to the whole, and the whole consists of the sum of the parts—causally speaking. But intentions certainly do not work this way. Groups regularly bring things about that none of their members plan, intend, or indeed even ever envision. Every cowboy just wants to kill his few buffalo—no one contemplates extermination of the species. There is no way to sum up individual intentions into an aggregate intention vis-à-vis the overall result. The denizens of the City of London rebuilt their city after the great fire of 1661, and the inhabitants of Charleston, South Carolina, did the same after the catastrophic destruction wrought by Hurricane Hugo in 1991. Collectively they accomplished the task, but distributively each property owner simply addressed the problems of his or her own case. Among those who were active in the rebuilding, virtually no one had any intentions in regard to the bigger object— the intentions of each were for the most part focused on the particular microtask at hand. The overall macroachievement lay outside the reach of anyone's intention. A group's interactively produced macroresults are all too frequently uncontemplated, unforeseen, unplanned, and even undesired by many, most, or even all of that group's individual members.

And so, while the responsibility or intention of groups must indeed derive from and inhere in that of its constituent individuals, it will actually do so only in special circumstances. The coordinative factor of an at least vicarious consent must be there, and in the absence of individual participation (of an at least statistical, majoritarian sort) there must at least be centralization through representation. The fact of the matter is that without an appropriate coordination of individual intentions it makes no sense to impute intention to a group.

It makes sense to say that a collectivity wants or intends something only when we have either

1. *consensual subscription*: when the macro-objective at issue is something that the generality or the substantial majority of group members want *as such*, thus rendering it into an object of the collective *volonté générale*, so to speak, or

2. *representative endorsement*: when the duly delegated representatives of the group's members duly agree to producing the result in question.

To be sure, distributive coincidence is not sufficient to yield the sort of intent at issue. The element of collectivity must be present. And there must be the right sort of coordination. The members of a board may distributively happen to be of one mind in all wanting the chairman dead, but this does not mean that the one who goes and shoots him is implementing a group consensus. Their "wanting him dead" does not come to "wanting him killed," let alone "wanting him killed by *X*." Here, those who have remained inert have certainly not "agreed" to the murder simply in view of their (perhaps reprehensible) attitude. The members may want him dead but do not agree to his being rendered so by the sort of action at issue. For collective responsibility the group must constitute something of a "moral person" with a collective unity of mind.

The conjunctivity at issue means that whenever group responsibility does in fact exist there must be responsible individuals: group responsibility cannot exist without individual responsibility. And this need for a proper grounding in the responsibility of individuals means that it cannot happen that a group does something wrong without there being culpable individuals at whose door some of the blame can be laid. (Note that it is crucial for the tenability of this statement that it reads "something *wrong*" and not merely "something *bad*.") Group responsibility must have a rooting in the responsibilities of individuals and cannot manage to exist without this. (It is not that groups cannot produce bad results without any individual member doing anything bad, but rather that when this happens, moral—as opposed to causal—responsibility cannot be laid anywhere. Moral culpability requires morally culpable individuals.)

All the same, collective responsibility is just exactly that—collective. It emphatically does *not* function distributively—it cannot automatically be projected upon the individuals who constitute that collectivity. We can indeed reason from "Tom, Dick, and Harry talked about mathematics" to "Tom and Dick talked about mathematics." But we can no more reason from "Tom, Dick, and Harry carried the piano upstairs" to "Tom and Dick carried the piano upstairs" than we can reason from "Tom, Dick, and Harry filled up the sofa" to "Tom and Dick filled up the sofa." Only in very special cases will the doings of collectivities project down to their component units.[2]

## 4. CONSEQUENCES FOR COLLECTIVE RESPONSIBILITY

With these considerations about causation and consent in mind, we can profitably return to our initial question. When the individual actions of diverse agents collectively issue in an overall result there is, by hypothesis, a collective causality in point of productivity. But does *moral* responsibility follow from this? Is there also automatically room for guilt and credit, praise and blame, laudation and reprehension?

Given the aforementioned complexities of collective intentionability the answer is clearly a negative here. For this reason, it would be folly to argue: The individually intentional actions of the members of a group produced a certain result, hence the members of the group are individually responsible for that result. Exactly as in the accidental overdosing case considered above, no single agent in a group whose acts are conjointly disastrous need do anything wrong or blameworthy.

Without the requisite coordination of individual intentions through consensus or delegative authorization it makes no sense to speak of group intentions. So-called guilt by association—by merely being a member of a group that collectively produces a bad result—is just not enough to establish a valid imputation of responsibility. In a bank run every depositor just wants his own money from the bank—no one foresees or intends the ruin and bankruptcy that ensues. But who is responsible? "Everybody and nobody," and so in the final analysis no one. Except in special conditions and circumstances—when the proper sort of coordination obtains—the intentions of individuals simply do not aggregate into some sort of group product: they do not somehow blend together into a group intention. And where intention is absent, there too responsibility is missing. When a group produces an unintended disaster, the situation as regards culpability is exactly the same as when an individual produces a wholly unintentional disaster—to wit there simply *is no culpability*. Without a normative responsibility that transcends mere causality, there can be no actual guilt. When this sort of thing happens, we can regret but cannot reproach.

The pivotal fact in this connection is that responsibility for the collective transgressions of a group can be projected down upon its component individuals only in special conditions. Only where group malfeasance indeed roots in the informed consent of individuals through coordination or delegation can those individuals be held to blame. And even then only subject to limits. To be culpable, individuals must form part of that consensus or be party to the consent. The defenses "I was opposed to it" and "I cast my vote against it" must be allowed their due weight in matters of individual exculpation.

Escaping group responsibility by dissociation is thus possible throughout the spectrum from explicit abstention to actual opposition. The ideological impetus of the ethically inspired resisters to Nazism is a case in point. Their actual efforts were futile and unavailing (perhaps often even incompetent). But symbolically they are of the greatest significance in providing a highly visible token of the fact that the German people as a whole did not go along here, so that an explicit line must be maintained between Germans and Nazis.

On the other hand, individuals can indeed be held responsible for group actions even if in a strict sense they didn't have anything to do with the malfeasance at issue. When their intentionability is betokened by way of consent or consensus, then those evil acts that a group's agents (few though they be) actually perform on behalf and under the consensual aegis of the wider group will also fall into the responsibility sphere of its individual members. Association is not enough to establish responsibility, but the sort of association involved in being an "accessory" of sorts—be it consensual or delegative—can prove sufficient. And even tacit consent can do so. The acquiescing citizenry is indeed responsible for the authorized actions of its duly delegated agents.

## 5. THE LEGAL ASPECT:
## MORAL VERSUS LEGAL RESPONSIBILITY

A thorny question now arises. If an appropriately structured coordinative basis in individual responsibility is indeed required for the moral responsibility of a group, then what of collectively produced outrages that are uncoordinated?

Two contrasting positions are possible here. At the one pole there is the "Protestant" position that individuals are the prime (perhaps even the sole!) bearers of responsibility. Here the position is that agents stand on their own feet in matters of evaluation appraisal. And so, when a group produces a collective result, then its individual agents are responsible only for their own individual acts—and so only for their free and intended individual contributions. They are responsible for and creditable with only those negativities and positivities that they themselves engender through their own suitably deliberate actions. Contextual considerations can be dismissed from the moral point of view. In practical effect, we can simply forget about the issue of group responsibility as a distinct issue: moral deliberation can be limited to the domain of individuals; group evaluations are at most statistical summaries.

At the other pole is the "Hebraic" position that the community is the prime (perhaps even the sole!) bearer of responsibility for collectively produced results—that what the group collectively does can and must be laid unavoidably at its collective door in point of responsibility. (To be sure, whether this collective responsibility can then be downloaded upon the constituent individual of the community still remains as an additional and potentially controversial question, but the responsibility of the community as a whole remains in any event—irrespective of how we answer this additional question.) In effect, the group is thus treated as a responsible individual in its own right in a way that is essentially independent of the responsibilities of its members. Groups are morally autonomous: they stand on a collective footing—the idea is simply rejected that the responsible actions of groups must inhere in or derive from their individual members.

We thus come to the question: As regards specifically *moral* responsibility, which is the right line to take here: the Protestant or the Hebraic? At this point the question of law versus ethics comes to the fore.

To start with, it deserves to be noted that in actual practice we generally allow legality and morality to go separate ways. And we do so for very practical reasons. Some examples will help to make this point.

Strictly speaking, the person who drives home drunk after the office party and has the good luck not to have an accident that injures others is in exactly the same *moral* position as the person who fails to be so lucky.[3] But *legally* there is all the difference in the world here: legally the one is (so we suppose) guilty while the other altogether guilt free. Here the legal standing of the two is thus very different. The law is concerned with actual results in a way that morality is not. Again, military law holds the commander responsible for mishaps for which there may well be no actual *causal* responsibility at the personal level. So here there will be situations where one will be morally innocent but legally culpable. And again, in group punishment situations, one charges the "innocent" members of the group with an onus of responsibility that has no moral basis. Here too the law can reflect the society's pragmatic care for results in a way that bypasses moral complications.

The fact is that the law is part of a system of social contract that has other fish to fry besides that of fixing moral culpability. And in consequence it often insists on beneficial overall results at the expanse of strict justice. The pivotal point is that legal and administrative systems embody a concern for certain social desiderata distinct from strict justice per se. This circumstance makes for a crucial difference between moral and legal responsibility.[4]

From the *moral* point of view the proper line will have to be that the source and basis of responsibility are always with individuals. Thus, moral responsibility belongs to groups only insofar as the individuals are suitably active within them. Groups can only bear responsibility derivatively—either by way of aggregation (consensus) or by way of delegation (via representation). And moral responsibility is in a way inalienable. It remains with those causally contributing individuals even when they transmit it to the group with which they act. But with *legal* responsibility, the situation is different. Groups can be *legal* persons and thus bear legal responsibility.

Legal responsibility is alienable and capable of transfer and delegation. Forming a corporation (or "legal person") or imposing a collective sanction on a criminal group or a destructive society makes perfectly good sense.

In this contrast between moral and legal responsibility we thus find a reflection of the contrast between the aforementioned Protestant and Hebraic positions on responsibility. And as far as *moral* wrongdoing is concerned, the Protestant position is surely plausible: the moral culpability of groups must inhere in that of its individuals—with the result that there can be collective acts that are unfortunate and regrettable, but yet not wrong, owing to the absence of any personal wrongdoing.

## 6. SOME LESSONS

An instructive lesson emerges from these deliberations. If as was insisted above, (1) the only avenue to group responsibility/reprehension is indeed via group intention, and moreover, (2) group intention requires coordination— either through an aggregation afforded by consensus or through a centralized delegation to representative deciders—then it follows that (3) there will unavoidably be many instances where group-engendered outrages will "fall between the stools" as far as responsibility and reprehension goes. And this means that there will thus be group-engendered catastrophes where responsibility admits of no specific allocation to individuals, since it is a merely fortuitous confluence of individual actions that does the mischief.

Who, then, can be held responsible for the carnage on America's roads, the poor performance of its schools, the decay of its social conscience and its public civility? Clearly only those who bear some sort of immediate responsibility. Reproaching the group as a whole makes no sense here, seeing that the requisite element of interpersonal coordination is lacking. Such aggregate negativities are the confluence of the uncoordinated and disjointed actions of innumerable individuals. They result from the causal contributions of many but the intentionality of none. And this lack of intentionality precludes the availability of actual culprits.[5]

Those aggregate effects that come to be realized through the vicissitudes of context lying beyond the ken and control of the individuals involved have to be viewed as "accidents of circumstance" with respect to which the chain of moral responsibility is severed en route to an aggregate causal result. As the case of the "Good Samaritan Mishap" illustrates, those terrible overall results have come about through the intentional doings of individuals alright, but there is nothing intentional about them *as such*. The only relevant intentions were fragmentary and disjointed—and so for this very reason were the responsibilities of individuals. Overall catastrophe was never envisioned—let alone intended—by anybody. The responsible actions of people produce disaster, alright, but a disaster that, as such, is detached from the responsibility of individuals (in any sense over and above the causal).

Thus, the perhaps unwelcome fact of the matter is that individually the actions of people can still be blameless—and perhaps praiseworthy—even in cases where the collective, combined result of their actions is a disaster. (The destabilizing rush of people to the side of the boat from which a cry of "save me" emanates is perhaps something of an example.) When such aggregated mishaps occur as a causal result of people's unconcerted actions, there is nothing for which that those disaggregated individuals can be held culpable. Here collective actions can engender aggregate outrages that are entirely culprit free as far as individual agents are concerned. The prospect of a lack of any suitable basis for attributing a communal intent means that the action of groups can sometimes produce terrible results for which there is neither collective responsibility nor individual fault.

What we have here is a fact of life that moral philosophy and common sense alike simply have to take in stride. In this regard, group causation is like nature causation—the group in effect acts like an irrepressible natural force rather than a personal agent. There is no sense in blaming the chair that we stumble over in the dark. When uncooperative nature produces a bad result, there simply is no one who can plausibly be asked to bear the burden of reproach. We regret the result but cannot find someone to blame for it. It is just "one of those #!@?* things" that we have to come to terms with in a difficult world. And much the same thing has to be said when unhappy aggregate effects come about through the disaggregated actions of members of a group. Morally, each individual can, should, and must bear responsibility for his or her own individual acts and intentions. But, to reemphasize, the aggregate effect—however unfortunate—may prove to be just one of those unfortunate things.

This, at least, is how matters stand from the moral point of view. And there is a significant lesson here. Causal and moral responsibility behave very differently in situations of collectivity. By hypothesis, an agent whose intended actions play a contributing part on the side of *causal* production will thereby and for this very reason bear a share of *causal* responsibility in relation to the overall product. But of course *moral* responsibility is not like that; it is not simply a matter of aggregation. Here the whole can be less than the sum of its parts—or more. No causal collective results can exist without individual causal contributions. But collective morally negative or positive results can indeed emerge in situations where individuals make no personal contributions of morally positive or negative coloration.

But what about group responsibility for faults of omission—for culpable inaction? The pivotal consideration here is a failure to act in the presence of opportunity, when this matter of opportunity pivots on (1) the existence of a suitable *occasion* where action is called for, (2) an *awareness* that this is so, be it by the group at large or those duly responsible for the conduct of its affairs, and (3) the availability of the requisite *means* for action. On this basis, the culpable inaction of groups is again something substantially analogous to the situation with regard to individuals. Still, when groups neglect doing something that they (morally speaking) ought to do—that is, to do *as a group*—can the blame for these omissions be laid at the doors of their individuals? The answer is yes, but, namely: *but only under special conditions* obtaining when that group neglect is the result of a culpable (or inexcusable) oversight on the part of individuals. If, as maintained above, it is indeed the case that group responsibility must inhere in individual responsibility and cannot exist without it, then this will also hold insofar as responsibility for omission is concerned. (Question: But just which individuals are responsible for the group's default? Answer: Exactly those whose intentionality was causally involved. Intentional causation is again the crux—absent the usual array of responsibility deflectors.)

## 7. A REVIEW OF THE ARGUMENT

The preceding deliberations, though brief, tell a rather complicated story. It is accordingly useful to pass the overall argument in review:

1. Responsibility presupposes (a) productive agent causality and (b) deliberate intentions.
2. The productive causality of groups can issue from the entirely disconnected and uncoordinated agency of its constituent individuals. There are accordingly two modes of group productivity: (a) the actually coordinated and (b) the uncoordinated and "accidentally" confluent as it were.
3. For the intentionality of group products there must be a coordinative synthesis of the individuals' intentions. Such coordinative cohesion can take two forms: the informally *consensual* or the formally *representational*. In the former case we have the explicit agreement of (at least most of) the members; in the latter case we have the imputed consent of the members at issue via the mediation of representational institutions.

4. Where the products of group activity are concerned, it only makes sense to speak of group intentions in the case of coordinated productions. Without the synthesis or unification of actions there is no meaningful collective intention.
5. An absence of intentionality means that group actions may be *disastrous* without there being any wrongdoing on the part of individuals.
6. However, group actions cannot be *wrong* in the absence of individual wrongdoing.
7. This is because intention—and thus responsibility—must initiate with individuals. Groups can achieve such a condition only "by derivation"—that is, via the mechanics of consensuality and/or delegated consent.
8. Accordingly, group intention/responsibility therefore exists only with coordinated group products produced under conditions of a synthesis of individual intentions via consensus or delegation. Then and only then is it proper to project group responsibility onto its component individuals—and only to the extent that their own intentions were causally involved.

## 8. CONSEQUENCES

One significant consequence of these deliberations is that group responsibility can lapse into nothingness where rogue regimes abrogate the normal processes of representative government. The people of Uganda cannot be held responsible for the excesses of Idi Amin's regime, nor the people of Russia for those of Stalin, whose transformations of governmental organism through state terrorism they neither foresaw nor endorsed. On the other hand, the responsibility of Americans for the atomic bombing of Japan in World War II or for the defoliation of crops and the destruction of villages in the Vietnam War cannot be denied—at any rate not on this basis of flawed intentionality. (But of course this collective responsibility of the group does not automatically authorize distribution upon its individual members.)

At this point an interesting question arises. For group intentions we have appealed to two coordinative factors: distributive consensus and centralized consent through representational institutions. But what if these two get out of joint with one pointing one way and the other another. What becomes of group responsibility when the group's legally constituted representatives act in the face of a general consensus to the contrary? For example, should one impute to the people of Britain credit for abolishing the death penalty or reprehension for tolerating fox hunting, seeing that Parliament's position on these issues is decidedly out of phase with the opinion polls?

There is—there can be—no simple answer here. What we have is yet another illustration of the fact that conceptual tidiness cannot be secured in a difficult world. In such situations we confront complex questions that require complex answers.

## 9. APPENDIX: COLLECTIVE CREDIT

The preceding deliberations have mainly taken into view the negative side of evaluative responsibility in regard to blame and guilt. But of course there is also the positive side of praise and credit. And it is—and should be—reasonably clear that the overall situation here must be seen as substantially analogous.

However, the analogy is not complete. An important and interesting difference arises. When several individuals actively collaborate in doing something bad (say, in a murder conspiracy), then each of them is standardly credited with—that is, bears legal and moral blame for—the production of that negative result: each of them is regarded as being guilty of murder.[6] But when individuals actively collaborate in the production of something good (say, in making a scientific discovery or in establishing a museum), then they are credited only with their own particular identifiable contribution. It would seem that the difference in treatment here lies in the practicalities of the matter rather than in purely abstractly theoretical considerations. We systematically seek to *discourage* individual participation in the doing of bad things and to *encourage* the efforts of individuals toward the doing of good. And these desiderata are clearly reflected in the disanalogy at issue.

Let us explore this aspect of the issue a bit further. Anyone who has ever worked on a crossword puzzle with a collaborator realizes that here the whole is greater than the sum of the parts—that the collaboration synergy of two working together is something superior to the mere compilation of their separate achievements. In such collaborative problem-solving situations we encounter the synergetic potentiation of teamwork. The work of one member helps to potentiate that of another. In joining forces the group members pave the way to an entirely new level of achievement. But in such cases to whom does the credit for this advancement—this "collaborative surplus"—belong?

It all depends. There are principally two kinds of teams: those that are leader directed and/or hierarchical and those that are purely cooperative and unstructured. In the former case matters of responsibility are again comparatively straightforward: responsibility and with it credit issues from the top down. But in the latter case there will be some diffusion. When individuals cooperate collectively in the production of something positive, the "surplus" of achievement over and above what individuals accomplish on their own will presumably be allocated in proportion to the extent to which they made their individual contributions. Such a principle once again provides for the maximum of reasonable encouragement.

## NOTES

I am grateful to my colleague David Gauthier for his constructive criticisms of a draft of this paper, which was initially published in the *Journal of Social Philosophy* 29 (1998): pp. 44–58. Reprinted by kind permission of the publisher.

1. Legal or institutional responsibility is something else again—something rather different from the ethical or moral. The captain is "responsible" for what happens on the ship; the officer is "responsible" for the acts of subordinates. But what is at issue here involves a rather different use of the term.

2. Compare G. J. Massey, "Tom, Dick, and Harry, and all the King's Men," *American Philosophical Quarterly* 13 (1976): pp. 89–107.

3. On this issue of "moral luck" see the author's treatment in *Luck* (New York: Farrar Straus Giroux, 1995).

4. On these issues see Nicholas Rescher and Carey B. Joynt, "Evidence in History and the Law," *The Journal of Philosophy* 56 (1959): pp. 561–78.

5. Note that so long as we refuse to project group responsibility onto the constituent individuals, then—even in the Hebraic case—we are confronted with the anomalous upshot that a group can, through the deliberate actions of the individuals involved, produce a terrible result for which as regards individuals no one is to blame through lack of the right sort of intent in the point of individuals.

6. To be sure, the presence of some degree of active participation is a crucial factor. Mere membership—wholly passive and inert—in a group that is collectively responsible does not as such contribute to the individual's moral blame or credit. And so the terrible things done by the Nazis at large detract nothing from the credit of Schindler, the Nazi.

# Conclusion

These pages have traversed a large and diversified terrain in the domain of rational decision issues. Above all, they have sought to establish the key role of evaluative and even moral considerations as integral components of this domain. Beyond that, the general tendency of these deliberations has been to explain and substantiate six key conclusions:

1. The issues of rational decision that confront us afford both an opportunity and an obligation that are unavoidable parts of the human condition.
2. Realization of this objective in the conditions that actually confront us can prove to be a very sophisticated and complex process that cannot be accomplished by ratiocinatory intelligence alone but also requires sensitive and sensible judgment in matters of evaluation.
3. Such evaluation is made difficult by involving not only personal aims and goals but also value facts that are impersonal, objective, and (all too often) also moral.
4. As coordinating the actions of individuals in a commonly benign way becomes more and more difficult in an increasingly complex world, considerations of impersonal reason in the light of collectively shared interests is to all appearances the most practicable and powerful means for meeting these needs.
5. While social consensus on public policy matters is doubtless a desideratum, it is inevitable to expect it in prevailing circumstances, so that domestic governance must devise acceptable ways and means of proceeding in its absence.
6. In matters of social decision the moral dimension of right and wrong and the correlative issue of responsibility are neither straightforward nor avoidable.

All in all, then, the book has sought to illustrate and substantiate the thesis that the evaluation of ends is an integral component of rationality as such and brings to light the problematic questionable nature of the view—all too popular among philosophers, economists, and decision theorists—that a consideration of means to desired ends suffices for the purposes of rational decision and that the inherent desirability of ends need be of no concern. In opposition to such a stance, the main thesis of these deliberations is that the decision problems posed in an era of technological sophistication do not admit of any merely technical resolution that can be developed in the absence of a concern for their evaluative and even moral ramifications.

# Bibliography

Arrow, Kenneth J. "Alternative Approaches to the Theory of Choice in Risk-Taking Situations." *Econometrica* 19 (1951): pp. 404–37.

——. *Essays on the Theory of Risk-Bearning.* Clarage: Morkham, 1971.

Axelrod, R., and W. D. Hamilton. "The Evolution of Cooperation." *Science* 211 (1981): pp. 1390–96.

Baier, Kurt. *The Moral Point of View.* Abridged ed. New York: Random House, 1965.

Bernoulli, Daniel. *Versuch einer neuen Theorie von Glücksfällen.* Translated by A. Pringsheim. Leipzig, 1896.

Campbell, Richmond, and Lanning Sowden, eds. *Paradoxes of Rationality and Co-operation.* Vancouver: University of British Columbia Press, 1985.

Descartes, René, *Discourse on Method.*

Earman, John. *Bayes or Bust.* Cambridge, Mass.: MIT Press, 1992.

Fairley, G. W. "Criteria for Evaluating the 'Small' Probability of a Catastrophic Accident from the Marine Transportation of Liquefied Natural Gas." In *Risk-benefit Methodology and Application: Some Papers Presented at the Engineering Foundation Workshop, Asilomar.* Edited by D Okrent. Los Angeles: University of California, Department of Energy and Kinetics, UCLA-ENG 7598; 1975.

Feyerabend, Paul K. *Against Method.* London and New York: Humanities Press, 1975.

Fischoff, Baruch. "Cost-benefit Analysis and the Art of Motorcycle Maintenance." *Policy Sciences* 8 (1977): pp. 177–202.

Green, A. E., and A. J. Bourne. *Reliability Technology.* New York: Wiley-Interscience, 1972.

Gutman, Mattias, et al., eds. *Kultur-Handlung-Wissenschaft.* Weiderwest: Velbrick Wissenschart, 2002.

Hayek, F. A. "The Theory of Complex Phenomena." In *Studies in Philosophy, Politics and Economics.* London: Routledge & Kegan Paul, 1967.

——. *The Counter-Revolution of Science: Studies on the Abuse of Reasons.* 2d ed. Indianapolis, Ind.: The Free Press, 1979.

Hobbes, Thomas. *De Cive.*

Holdren, J. P. "The Nuclear Controversy and the Limitations of Decision Making by Experts." *Bulletin of the Atomic Scientists* 32 (1976): pp. 20–22.

Jeffrey, Richard. *The Logic of Decision.* 2d ed. Chicago and London: University of Chicago Press, 1983.

Kates, R. W. "Hazard and Choice Perception in Flood Plain Management." Research Paper No. 78, Department of Geography, University of Chicago, 1962.

Kekes, John. *Justification of Rationality.* Albany: SUNY Press, 1976.

Kluckhohn, Clyde. "Ethical Relativity; Sic et non." *The Journal of Philosophy* 52 (1955): pp. 663–77.

———. *Culture and Behavior.* Glencoe, Ill.: The Free Press, 1962.

Kohl, H. R. *The Age of Complexity.* New York: New American Library, 1965.

Kyburg, Henry E., Jr. *Probability and the Logic of Rational Belief.* Middletown, Conn.: Wesleyan University Press, 1961.

Lewis, David. "Causal Decision Theory." *Australasian Journal of Philosophy* 59 (1981).

Linton, Ralph. "Universal Ethical Principles: An Anthropological View." In *Moral Principles of Action.* Edited by R. N. Anshen. New York: Harper, 1952.

———. "The Problem of Universal Values." in *Method and Perspective in Anthropology.* Edited by R. F. Spencer. Minneapolis: University of Minnesota Press, 1954.

Lowrance, William W. *Of Acceptable Risk.* Los Allos: Kaufmann, 1976.

Mainzer, Klaus. *Thinking in Complexity: The Complex Dynamics of Matter, Mind, and Mankind.* Berlin: Springer Verlag, 1994.

Massey, G. J. "Tom, Dick, and Harry, and all the King's Men." *American Philosophical Quarterly* 13 (1976): pp. 89–107.

Nozick, Robert. "Newcomb's Problem and Two Principles of Choice." In *Essays in Honor of Carl G. Hempel.* Edited by N. Rescher. Dordrecht: D. Reidel, 1969.

Parkinson, C. Northcote. *Parkinson's Law.* Boston: Houghton Mifflin, 1957.

Perrow, Charles. *Normal Accidents Living with High-Risk Technologies.* New York: Basic Books, 1984.

Popper, K. R. *Conjectures and Refutations: The Growth of Scientific Knowledge.* New York: Harper Torchbooks, 1965.

Poundstone, W. *Labyrinths of Reason.* New York: Andiron-Doubleday, 1990.

Pralt, J. W. "Risk Aversion in the Small and the Large." *Econometrics* 32 (1964): pp. 122–36.

Redfield, R. "The Universally Human and the Culturally Variable." *The Journal of General Education* 10 (1967): 150–60.

Rescher, Nicholas, and Carey B. Joynt. "Evidence in History and the Law." *The Journal of Philosophy* 56 (1959): pp. 561–78.

Rescher, Nicholas. *Essays in Philosophical Analyses.* Pittsburgh: University of Pittsburgh Press, 1969.

———. *The Coherence Theory of Truth.* Oxford: Oxford University Press, 1973.

———. *Risk.* Lanham, Md.: University Press of America, 1983.

———. *Forbidden Knowledge.* Dordrecht: Kluwer, 1987.

———. *Rationality.* Oxford: Clarendon Press, 1988.

———. *The Validity of Values.* Princeton, N.J.: Princeton University Press, 1993.

——. *Luck.* New York: Farrar-Straus-Giroux, 1995.

——. *Complexity.* Transaction Publishers, 1998.

Rosenberg, Alexander. *Philosophy of the Social Science.* Boulder, Colo.: Westview Press, 1988; 2d ed. 1995.

Rosenthal, Josh. "Looking Forward, Looking Back: The New York Times Magazine 1896-1996-2096." *The New York Times Magazine*, September, 29, 1996, pp. 45–46.

Scriven, Michael. "An Essential Unpredictability in Human Behavior." In *Scientific Psychology*. Edited by B. B. Wolman. New York: Basic Books, 1965.

Simon, Herbert. *Models of Bounded Rationality.* 3 vols. Cambridge, Mass.: MIT Press, 1997.

Slote, Michael A. *Beyond Optimizing.* Cambridge, Mass.: Harvard University Press, 1989.

Slovic, Paul. "Behavioral Decision Theory." *Annual Review of Psychology* 28 (1977): pp. 1–39.

Slovic, Paul, et al. "Preference for Insuring against Probable Small Losses: Insurance Implications." *The Journal of Risk and Insurance* 44 (1977): pp. 237–58.

Thomson, Judith Jarvis. *The Realm of Rights.* Cambridge, Mass.: Harvard University Press, 1990.

Tversky, A., and D. Kahneman. "Judgment under Uncertainty: Heuristics and Biases." *Science* 185 (1974): pp. 1124–31.

U.S. Atomic Energy Commission [U.S. Nuclear Regulatory Commission]. *An Assessment of Accident Risks in U.S. Commercial Nuclear Power Plants.* Washington, D.C., 1974.

U.S. Food and Drug Administration. "Chemical Compounds in Food-processing Animals. Criteria and Procedures for Evaluating Assays of Carcinogenic Residues." Washington, D.C.; March 20, 1979; 44 Federal Register, 17070–17114.

Wolf, Susan. "Two Levels of Pluralism." *Ethics* 102 (1992): pp. 785–98.

# Name Index

# About the Author

Nicholas Rescher is University Professor of Philosophy at the University of Pittsburgh. He is a former president of the American Philosophical Association and president-elect of the American Catholic Philosophical Association. He is the author of more than one hundred books encompassing many areas of philosophy.